The Cabin Crew Interview Made Easy
Everything you need to know about being successful at a Flight Attendant interview

By Caitlyn Rogers

WITHDRAWN

CE PUBLISHING™
www.cepublishing.org

The Cabin Crew Interview Made Easy

Everything you need to know about being successful at a Flight Attendant interview

By Caitlyn Rogers

Copyright © 2006 CE Publishing and Caitlyn Rogers
Registration number 262514

This work is registered with the UK Copyright Service

A catalogue record for this book is available from the British Library.

First edition 2006

ISBN   978-0-9552818-3-9

CE Publishing
info@cepublishing.org
http://www.cepublishing.org

This book is available at quantity discounts for bulk purchases
Please visit www.cepublishing.org for further information

CONTENTS

Part 1 The Application Process

Part 2 The Interview Process

Part 2a Questions and Answers

Part 2b Forms

Introduction

Over 90% of all candidates who attend a Cabin Crew interview fail without making it through the first round, and its getting worse. It's just ridiculous!

But how can this be? With all those books and websites out there dedicated to telling you about this very subject, how come so many people still suffer the dreaded outcome? And more importantly, how can you be certain that you're not going to be one of these 90% who fail?

Well, provided you're armed with the correct knowledge of how to be successful, you can be successful first time.

The bad news however, is that until now, there was nothing available to provide you with this knowledge! Because all those books and websites out there all share one common problem, they focus on what you will be doing when and if you get the job and how to pass the training rather than 'What it actually takes and What exactly you need do to pass the interview'.

So what can be done about this shocking state of affairs?

Well my friend, this is where this book comes in... 'The Cabin Crew Interview Made Easy' is unlike any other book available... You will discover precisely what will separate you from the thousands of others, and get specific, no holds barred Cabin Crew Interview advice.

'The Cabin Crew Interview Made Easy' will take you through the whole process – from putting the paperwork together to answering the toughest questions.

This book is written in two interconnected parts, 'The Application Process' which will provide examples of how to fill in the application form for maximum impact, compose a cover letter and resume that will demand attention and create professional photographs that will give the impression of cabin crew material .

Once you are ready for action, 'The Interview Process' takes you through simple and effective ways to ensure that you have a successful interview, from the moment you leave your home to the moment the interview finishes.

Here you will discover what can be expected during the group interview and how you can demonstrate both the desired traits and skills necessary for cabin crew. Here, you will also find hundreds of the toughest, sneakiest and, meanest questions that recruiters love to throw at you. With each question will be a full length sample answer, which can be adapted and customised to your individual circumstances. With over 300 full length detailed answers provided and a formula to follow for creating your own answers, you will be fully prepared for any eventuality.

I will also disclose the best kept secret behind the selection process... The reason why 90% of all candidates are unsuccessful and have no idea why. Not only will I disclose this secret, I will also advise how you can use the information to your advantage.

Read this book and arm yourself with the advantage of knowing what interviewers are looking for and how you can supply it.

Part 1

The Application Process

In this part...

How to fill in the application form for maximum impact, compose a cover letter and resume that will demand attention and create professional photographs that will give the impression of cabin crew material.

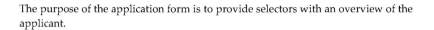
The purpose of the application form is to provide selectors with an overview of the applicant.

Selectors will use the form to formulate the most appropriate questions to ask at the interview, explore a candidate's motives and also screen out unsuitable candidates without having to go to the expense of inviting them to attend an interview.

The reasons why a candidate may be screened out at this stage are as follows...

- **Eligibility criteria** – If a candidate doesn't meet the eligibility criteria set by the airline, the candidate will not be invited to attend an interview. The eligibility criteria can include customer service experience, languages, age and/or level of education. *Before applying to any airline, you should check the airlines criteria to ensure that you meet those criteria.*

- **Messy, unreadable and badly completed application forms** – Your application form should be completed carefully and neatly. Write all your answers in pencil before you even attempt to fill it in with a pen so that any mistakes made can be easily rectified. It doesn't look professional if there are lots of liquid paper marks on the form.

> Use only black ink to complete your application form
> Make sure your handwriting is clearly legible, use block capitals
> Keep your answers within the boxes provided

As with any job, you want to ensure that you list the relevant skills and experience you have gained in your current or previous employment and match these as much as possible to the role of Cabin Crew.

Airlines are interested in your character. They look at the types of jobs you have held, for how long you worked for each and your reasons for leaving. They look at your educational achievements and any other self improvement attempts you have made to improve yourself. For this reason, include any volunteer or charity work you have carried out, awards you have received, and first aid courses you have taken.

Many Cabin Crew application forms will ask for some form of self-appraisal. A common example would be: "What qualities do you have that you feel will make you a good cabin crew member?" or "Please briefly relate a recent experience where you were especially pleased with the service/assistance you were able to give someone" This information provides selectors with an insight into candidate's motives and perceptions, and can sometimes be used to compliment observations made at the interview. *(Example answers to these sorts of questions can be found in the section Interview Questions and Answers)*

The contact details and permission to contact referees may also be requested. If reference details are requested, it is a good idea to provide them. *Make sure that you first receive permission from the person(s) you state as your referee(s)*

Depending upon the airline, application forms usually take between two weeks to three months to process (it has been known to be longer!). Those who are successful at this stage are then invited to attend a preliminary selection process.

DANGER: Be prepared!!

Upon submitting your application, if you are selected as a possible candidate, you may get a phone call out of the blue at the airlines discretion. If you do get a phone call, this will often be the start of the application process as apposed to asking you to attend an interview.

They will ask you a series of questions in relation to their target areas of interest/criteria relating to the position.

The outcome as to whether you go further and be invited to an interview or not is subject to your answers right there and right then!

Tip: Know the criteria that they will be assessing you against. Be friendly, speak clearly and address their questions as if you were in an interview! (Because you are; it just happens to be casually over the phone)!

Most airlines will ask for a recent photograph. **Candidates should make sure they send a good one.** This is the first stage in the personal presentation specification, so it is important to make a good impression. Selectors see many candidates in a day, and are constantly writing notes, so the photograph may well be referred to as a visual reminder.

Don't send casual holiday shots; Have your photos professionally taken - some airlines are so strict about the standard of the photographs that they may not even invite you to attend an interview unless you send professional photos.

As cabin crew, you will be the face of the airline and your standards of presentation should therefore be very high. With this in mind, I would suggest wearing something similar to a cabin crew uniform (don't be too obvious though, no scarf etc.). Most importantly, you must be smiling. This gives the impression that you are friendly and welcoming

For the ladies, make up is usually part and parcel with the cabin crew uniform, so wear plenty whilst still looking as natural as possible. Don't go overboard but emphasise your cheeks, lips and eyes. It's amazing what a bit of lipstick and blusher can do!

As for your hair, it should be neat and well groomed. For ladies, unless you have short hair, I would suggest pinning your hair back. Male candidates should have short but not shaved hair, and be clean shaven.

By following these suggestions, you will be maximising your opportunity for success because the person seeing the photos will be able to visualise you as cabin crew material.

See the following page for a good example of how you should be presenting yourself in your photographs.

Hair should be neat and tidy with no loose strands covering the face.

Plenty of make-up to cover any blemishes and make features stand out.

Professional looking suit.

Good upright posture with both hands visible. (Ensure nails are well manicured).

Posture (including legs and arms) straight.

Clean and tidy court shoes

It is also advised that you use a plain background in a colour that compliments your attire.

The Cover Letter

If you are applying to an airline via sending your resume, then the cover letter is a big chance to sell yourself; if you don't sell yourself in the cover letter, the person receiving your application, may not get to read your resume, you must give them a reason to continue reading.

Try to stick to one page so that reading it doesn't seem like a large task and try to leave plenty of white space around the page so that it doesn't appear overloaded.

Begin by first explaining your reason for contacting the airline. I would then suggest that you go on to explain a little bit about your experience and why you are seeking to become cabin crew. With a new paragraph, go on to tell them a little bit about yourself; what you can offer, your skills, etc.

Now it is time to close the letter. State that you have enclosed your resume and photographs and would welcome the opportunity to meet with them to discuss the opportunity further. Finished….

Although you want to give them a reason to continue reading, you don't want to show all your winning cards at once. The object is to give them a taster of what's to come whilst leaving yourself plenty more winning hands for the interview.

A good example of the perfect cover letter is on the following page. If you send something similar to the example shown, you will be giving a very good first impression of yourself without giving too much away.

JANE DOE

16 Any Road • Any Where
Manchester • AN8 9SE
United Kingdom
(+44) 04587 875848 • janedoe@anymail.com

XYZ Airline   12th October 2006
Cabin Crew Recruitment
43 Any Road
London
SW3 7KD

Dear sir/madam.

I would like to express my strong interest in the position of Cabin Crew.

I currently work as a freelance hairdresser and have worked in client-facing roles for more than 8 years. I am looking for a change in my life direction and feel that a career as cabin crew would give me this.

I am a friendly, approachable person and am able to work on my own initiative and as a team player. I am a people person and would deliver excellent customer service to passengers of all levels. I am a patient person who is able to stay professional and calm under pressure. I feel with my personality and experience I would be a valuable asset to XYZ Airlines.

A copy of my resume and photographs are enclosed for your consideration. Should you require further information, please feel free to contact me.

I would welcome the opportunity to meet with you to discuss this position and my background in more detail, and to explore the ways I could contribute to the ongoing success of your airline.

I appreciate your consideration and look forward to hearing from you.

Yours faithfully,

Jane Doe
Encl

The Perfect Resume

Different countries may have different requirements and styles for resumes. So you must follow the correct practice for your culture and country. However, we will try to give you important principles and advice.

Your resume is a very important document; imagine your resume as being a brochure that will list the benefits of a particular service. The service being your skills and experience!

The resume may be the only piece of information about you that an airline has. Your resume therefore has to represent the best you have to offer if you don't want to miss out on the job that is perfect for you.

Your resume is not only useful for getting you the interview but can continue to work in your favour at the interview by carefully focusing the interviewer's mind on your good points and your achievements. Therefore, straight away, your resume determines how your image is presented and it will influence the nature and direction of the interview. If your resume is strong, the interviewer will ask questions based on information that presents your image strongly.

Your resume should be an accurate record of your work history. Do not fabricate dates or leave companies out, and be sure to account for lapses in time.

Keep it short, no more than two pages in length - no one reads long resumes, they are boring!

Because many airlines are now using automated resume tracking systems, you should compile a resume that will be pleasant to the human eye, whilst also being computer friendly.

By computer friendly, I mean buzzwords. Buzzwords are words that are related to the job, for example... teamwork, customer care etc. The computer conducts a search for these buzzwords and then produces an overall score. The score represents your suitability and can be the difference between being invited for an interview or not.

resume

A human friendly resume will not be too lengthy, but not too packed in either.

Employers do not have the time to spare working out what your resume is trying to tell them. You must communicate clearly and concisely the information that you wish to convey about yourself that will be of relevance to them.

It is important that the headings (including your name) are clearly visible to make your resume easy to navigate. The order of your resume is also important; you want the most important information such as personal information, objective, key skills and strengths and present employment to be on the first page. Hobbies and interests, education and training and languages, whilst also important, can be left to the second page.

You can provide details of your referees or simply state that 'references are available on request', this is something that is entirely personal preference.

For a good example of a perfect resume, please see the following page.

JANE DOE

16 Any Road • Any Where • Any Town AN8 9SE • United Kingdom
(+44) 04587 875848 • janedoe@anymail.com

PERSONAL PROFILE

I currently work as a Freelance Hairdresser and have worked in client-facing roles for more than 8 years. I am looking for a change in my life direction and feel that a career as Cabin Crew would give me this. I am a people person and would deliver excellent customer service to passengers of all levels. I feel with my experience I would be a valuable asset to XYZ Airline.

KEY SKILLS AND STRENGTHS

Ability to work well with a variety of people on a constant basis • Ability to remain calm and organised in a pressured environment • Focused on quality customer care • Likeable and enthusiastic • Thrive in atmosphere of challenge and variety • Unaffected by working unsociable hours • Effective interpersonal communication skills • Good judgement and ability to make effective decisions

PERSONAL INFORMATION

Nationality: British
Marital Status: Single
Health: Excellent

Date of Birth: 21 May 1980
Availability: Immediate
Weight in proportion to height

EMPLOYMENT HISTORY

Freelance Hairdresser   **01 February 2003 – Present**
Working freelance, I have a broad range of responsibilities. In addition to the hairdressing service, I am also responsible for holding consultations, advising clients on suitable styles and/or treatments, ordering, and maintenance of stock, attending to telephone enquiries, calculating client bills and collecting payments, providing a point of sale for retail goods, keeping up to date records of accounts, establishing and maintaining relationships with clients, analysing and responding to feedback.

Any Hair Salon

Senior Stylist   **16 August 2000 – 01 February 2003**

As a senior stylist, my day to day duties included washing, cutting and styling hair, advising clients on suitable styles and/or treatments, holding consultations, providing aftercare and styling advice and supervising and training work experience students.

Junior Stylist   **05 April 1998 – 16 August 2000**

Serving as a member of a team, my day to day duties included washing, cutting and styling hair, advising clients on hair care, holding consultations with clients and providing aftercare and styling advice.

Receptionist   **24 July 1996 – 05 April 1998**

As a receptionist, my day to day duties included attending to enquiries, phasing appointments to ensure allocation of work in a way that is manageable by the hairstylists, ensuring the comfort of the clients while they wait, calculating client bills and collecting payments, cashing up at close of trading and providing a point of sale for retail goods.

EDUCATION AND TRAINING

Secondary Education   **Qualifications**
Any High School 1991 – 1996   11 GCSE's (grade A–D)

Training   **Awards**
Any College 1997 - 1998   NVQ 1 - Hairdressing
Any College 1998 – 1999   NVQ 2 - Hairdressing
Any College1999 – 2001   NVQ 3 - Hairdressing
Any College 2001   Certificate in Creative Cutting

LANGUAGES

Fluent in English • Knowledge of conversational French • Currently learning Spanish

HOBBIES & INTERESTS

Badminton • Reading • Yoga • Travelling • Hiking • Swimming • Cycling •

Written References Available Upon Request.

Part 2

Part 2

The Interview Process

In this part...

Preparing for the interview
Appearance and Etiquette
What airlines look for
The group interview
The secrets revealed...
Aptitude tests
The final interview
Leave a positive lasting impression
Questions & Answers

If you have been invited to attend the preliminary selection process, *Congratulations*... The fact that you have been invited to attend an assessment day means that the airline sees you as a competitive candidate and would like to learn more about you.

You now need to ensure you maximise your chances of being offered the position by showing the recruiters that you have what it takes to be a great Cabin Crew member.

This section discusses how to prepare for the interview.

- **Research the Airline**
  This is to ensure you tick the box for 'at least he/she did their homework and found out a bit about the Airline'. Visit the Airline's web site, read company literature, financials and press releases to find out about its mission statement, competitors, routes, awards, history & future plans, culture, values, size and reputation.

- **Prepare for and anticipate potential questions**
  It is a good idea to try to anticipate the questions that may be asked of you. Prepare answers beforehand to some of the more difficult or sensitive questions by practicing aloud or with a friend. *(See Interview Questions and Answers on pages 63-169 for examples of appropriate answers to many of the questions you may be asked)*

- **Draw up a list of questions to ask the interviewers**
  The questions you ask will reveal a lot about your level of interest in the Airline and your preparedness for the interview. Don't ask questions that could be easily answered through your own research. Instead ask questions which demonstrate a genuine interest in and knowledge of the Airline and the position. *(See Questions for the interviewers on page 169 for a list of examples)*

- **Refresh your maths knowledge**
  Some airlines require candidates to do a short maths test. If you are a little rusty, it is advisable that you refresh yourself on the basics (division, multiplication and currency conversion). *(See pages 44-49 for further information)*

- **Practice answering questions aloud**
As I mentioned previously, practicing answering your answers aloud to yourself or with a friend will benefit you a great deal and enhance your performance in a number of ways...

Even when you know how you would like to answer certain questions, it is not always easy to do it in practice (especially if you have not experienced an interview situation for some time). When questions are coming in quick succession (especially questions like "How did that make you feel?"), it can create an overload, and you may freeze up or find that you cannot articulate your answers as well as you would like. Practicing your answers and interview technique beforehand may help to prevent this.

- **Practice relaxation techniques**
Performing relaxation techniques before an interview can help calm your nerves. Deep breathing is the best relaxation technique, especially if you suffer from 'butterflies in your stomach'. When we are nervous, our breathing becomes shallow, deep breathing helps to get your breathing back on track.

- **Rehearse positive body language**
Body language conveys all sorts of messages and the right body language will convey the message of a well-balanced confident individual, even if you are not.

Rehearsing your body language will enable you to subconsciously continue using the body language whilst in the interview. Walking and sitting with a book on your head, on a regular basis, will over time help to straighten your posture.

- **Practice dealing with a difficult person**
Cabin crew are required to deal with difficult people on a regular basis and so the recruiters may put you on the spot and request you to carry out a short role play whereby the interviewer will play the role of a difficult customer.

Try getting a friend to help you practice by performing short role plays based around various scenarios that you may encounter aboard an aircraft.

- **Practice reading from unknown literature**
Many airlines will require you to read something aloud, especially during the group interview. If this is something that makes you feel uncomfortable, practice reading aloud to a group of friends or with a Dictaphone.

- **If you have a second language or English is not your native language, prepare for any tests**
If you are going to be required to take a language test, it is advisable to prepare in advance. In particular, ensure you have a reasonable vocabulary of words associated with aircraft, airports and passenger service. *(See page 53 for further information)*

- **Ensure that you know the correct interview location**
It is advisable to visit the location in advance to familiarise yourself with the route, parking and time it will take to get there so that you don't find yourself lost or late on the day. If for any reason you are unable to visit the location in advance, there are many useful resources on the internet that can provide you with detailed route maps including the distance.

THE DAY BEFORE YOUR INTERVIEW

- **Travelling arrangements**
If travelling by car, ensure in advance that your car has plenty of petrol in it and that you have change in your pocket for parking meters. Also check the road traffic reports. If travelling by public transport check times of trains/buses.

TAKE TO THE INTERVIEW

- **2 pens**
This is a necessity; you will likely want or be required to take note of something. Nothing looks more disorganised than if you have to ask someone to borrow a pen. At least two pens are crucial; one can be used as a backup should the other run out of ink or if the need arises, you can lend one to another candidate.

- **A pencil and eraser**
Both a pencil and eraser are important tools to carry to a Cabin Crew interviews. You may be required to carry out a maths test or complete a personality questionnaire, also known as psychometric test. You may want to complete the test in pencil the first time around so that any mistakes made can be easily rectified. You wouldn't want to be handing in your completed form with lots of scribbles over it.

- **A calculator**
  Carry a calculator in your bag should the need to use it arise.

- **A notepad**
  This goes without saying, you will most likely wish to take note of something and a notepad is tidier than lots of pieces of paper that may get lost.

- **A wrist watch**
  Returning back from your breaks on time is vital, you do not want to be relying on other people or wall clocks to tell you the time.

- **Documentation**
  I would suggest you carry 3 resumes with you, this includes one for yourself, and two extra copies just in case only one or none of the interviewers has a copy. Also take along your interview invitation, and any documentation that has been requested (passport, exam certificate, language certificate, references etc.).

- **1 portrait photo and 1 full length photo**
  You may have already sent these along with your application, but it is always good to have spares.

- **Hand cream, Mouth spray and Deodorant**
  These items will keep you feeling fresh throughout the day and keep you smelling good also.

- **A bottle of water and a light snack**
  The interviews can be long and gruelling; you will need a light refreshment when you get short break periods.

- **Cosmetics (foundation, face powder, eyeliner and lipstick)**
  Working as cabin crew, you are always expected to be well groomed, even after a long 14 hour shift. This means that you should be well groomed throughout the interview. Whenever you get a short bathroom break, ensure you touch up any areas needed.

- **An umbrella**
  You don't want to arrive soaked from head to toe.

BEFORE SETTING OFF

- **Set out with plenty of time to spare**
  Allow extra travelling time to account for delays in travel. Arriving at an interview late means you already start the interview from behind the rest of the candidates. It gives the impression that you can't organise yourself and plan. Better to be an hour early than a minute late. You can always grab a coffee and go through your notes. It also reduces the panic that could set in if you arrive in a hurry and aren't relaxed.

- **Have a light snack.**
  You will need energy for the day and it can be embarrassing and distracting if your stomach is rumbling during an interview.

- **Watch the news.**
  This is essential as you may be required to talk about current events, either during a group discussion or in the final 2 on 1 interview.

BEFORE ENTERING THE INTERVIEW ROOM

- **Take several deep breaths.**
  This will help calm your nerves and is best done standing. Inhale slowly, breathing through your nose, and try to fill your lungs completely. After a count of three, slowly exhale through your mouth. Concentrate on expelling all the air that you took in. You should see your stomach move out each time you breathe in, and flatten each time you breathe out. Feel your shoulders relax as you breathe out. Repeat this deep breathing four or five times.

During the first few minutes of an interview, the recruiters makes certain judgments about your character and work style based on your dress, demeanour and body language.

As cabin crew, you will be the face of the airline and your standards of presentation should therefore be very high. The airline wants to feel confident that you will present a polished, friendly and conservative image.

FEMALES

Dress
You cannot go wrong wearing a smart suit as it will make you appear more professional. Choose something that is well tailored and something that doesn't crease easily. Above all, wear something you feel good wearing.

Don't be afraid to introduce colour into your outfit... Most applicants will wear black, grey and navy blue and so by wearing another colour such as cream, pink or pale blue, you will instantly stand out from the crowd.

Tights/Stockings
Even in summer months, it is critical that you wear tights or stockings in order to create a sophisticated image.

Makeup
Makeup is usually part and parcel with the cabin crew uniform, so wear plenty whilst still looking as natural as possible. Don't go extreme but emphasise your cheeks, lips and eyes. It's amazing what a bit of lipstick and blusher can do!

Shoes
Wear conservative court shoes that are well polished and smart looking – no scuffed edges or tatty heels.

Hair
Your hair should be neat, freshly washed and well groomed. If you have long hair, don't feel you are required to wear it up for the interview. If the recruiters want to see how you look with your hair put up, they will ask you to sweep it back.

If you do wear your hair up, make sure there are no strands or straggly bits sticking out.

If you have coloured or bleached hair, make sure it looks natural... No root re-growth or funky/abnormal colours.

Hands & Nails
Ensure that your nails are tidy and not too long. Nail polish should be conservative and match in colour. Avoid charms, glitter and multi-coloured polish

MALES

Dress

Choose something that is of good quality, well tailored and fits well. Select a shirt that looks crisp, clean and smart. Try to avoid any fabrics that crease easily…

Wear a tie that portrays your personality yet is suitable for the formal occasion.

Shoes

Ensure shoes are clean, tidy and well polished.

Hair

Your hair should be well styled and freshly washed. Coloured or bleached hair should be natural looking with no root re-growth. Avoid outrageous colours or styles.

Facial Hair

Male Cabin Crew are not normally permitted to have beards so it is recommended that you attend the interview cleanly shaven. If you must have facial hair, it must be closely trimmed.

Hands & Nails

Ensure that your nails are tidy and short – not bitten.

MALES AND FEMALES

Perfume/Cologne
If you choose to wear perfume/cologne, select a light scent and wear it sparingly.

Jewellery/Body Piercings
Jewellery should be minimal and conservative. Wear no more than one ring per hand. Avoid cloth or rope bracelets and thumb rings.

Facial piercing is not acceptable – If you do have these, remove them before your interview

Tattoos
Visible tattoos are not acceptable. If you do have them, cover them up if possible.

Poise
Your poise should make you appear confident but welcoming, so walk and stand tall and retain open gestures.

Smile
Most importantly, you must smile, thus giving the impression that you are friendly and welcoming

By following the above guidance, you will be maximising your opportunity for success...

> **Note:**
> It's a mistaken belief that airlines only seek cabin crew who look like supermodels. They are looking for the whole package... behaviour, body language and necessary skills/qualifications

Put simply, Airlines are looking for the right people for their current circumstances. All Airlines have their own unique requirements so do not be disheartened if you are not successful at the first attempt. You can always try again or apply to another airline.

In making a decision about the employment of cabin crew, all airlines consider three key elements: Eligibility, Suitability and Specific Requirements... Put together these three elements form a 'Person Specification' which recruiters use to determine if a candidate is suitable or not.

ELIGIBILITY

Eligibility checks are based on facts that can be determined either by physical or documentary evidence.

Eligibility checks are likely to include:

- Does the candidate have a passport?
- Does the passport allow the candidate to fly to all the countries the airline operates to?
- Has the candidate passed the airline's 'in house' psychometric /numeracy /literacy/general knowledge tests?
- Can the candidate swim?

An airline may also have additional eligibility checks depending upon its own specific requirements. These may include:

- Does the candidate meet the required age profile?
- Does the candidate meet the required height/weight profile?
- Has the candidate attained the required educational qualifications?
- Has the candidate acquired adequate experience in a customer service or public contact role?
- Can the candidate speak a second language?
- To what level of proficiency can the second language be spoken?

Not all airlines are the same, so in order to avoid disappointment candidates are recommended to investigate eligibility criteria carefully before applying to an airline.

SUITABILITY

Unlike eligibility which is based on facts, suitability involves identifying the right personal qualities.

To summarise, the minimum requirement is for reliable, honest and presentable individuals, who can interact well with people, provide a service in a friendly way, work as part of a team and have the ability to cope under pressure.

Airlines will also be looking for people whose performance will not be negatively affected by the disadvantages of the job and will readily accept direction and training.

SPECIFIC REQUIREMENTS

Eligibility and Suitability are basic requirements, which must be met in all cases. Airlines then proceed to customise their specific requirements according to their own needs and standards.

If for example an airline identifies that an increase in the number of language speakers is required, then language ability may be given precedence. A good customer service background, nursing experience, or educational qualifications may be more relevant to one airline than to another.

Some airlines see above average appearance/presentation as being crucial, whilst others prefer a higher degree of charisma and personality. A new airline starting up may choose previous cabin crew experience as a prime requisite where as a prestigious and well established airline can often afford to be even more particular, and demand a combination of preferred attributes.

Once all the considerations are taken into account, the person specification is complete. These different considerations help to explain why some people are successful with one airline, and yet get rejected by another (their performance is obviously another factor!).

It is also true that some candidates fail to be recruited by an airline at one attempt, and then succeed at a later date. This is usually because the candidate has acquired better interview technique or extra skills, experience or confidence. It can also be because the airline itself has revised its person specification.

The following elements of the group interview process outlines only what is common to some airlines. As the exercises airlines choose are incredibly diverse and are frequently changed, not all elements will be included, and the sequence in which they are carried out is likely to vary.

The group interview is an opportunity for the recruiters to see how you adapt to meeting new people, working in a team as well as giving a true impression of each candidate's true personality.

Many of these scenarios have no right or wrong solution. Your actions show the interviewers how well you think on your feet and apply common sense in your solutions.

GROUP DISCUSSION

Here are a few examples of common topics you may encounter...

- For 15 minutes, discuss your ideas and opinions about the ban on public smoking.
- Think of 10 items you would take to survive a year on a tropical island.
- Discuss which ten famous people from world history you would invite to a dinner party and why?

The most important thing to bear in mind is that the topic is irrelevant! It is involvement, behaviour and personality which are really being assessed and how these qualities are applied in relation to the group. The recruiters will be assessing how much you participate, how well you listen and what part you play in the group.

GROUP EXERCISE

The usual format is for the group to be split into smaller teams to carry out these tasks.

Here are some examples of the types of exercises you may come across...

- With the materials provided (i.e. paper, selotape and scissors), design and build a strong bridge that will support a full roll of selotape.

- Using the pack of cards provided (the pack of cards may include various pictures such as paper cups, polo mints, ball of string etc...), discuss how you would use each of the items to entertain a group of passengers if you were stranded on a desert island. At the end of 20 minutes, you must present back to the recruiters what you have chosen and why.

- In 15 minutes, write a song that will advertise the airline. Then perform the song to the group. (You may be required to perform the song individually or as a group)

You may also be requested to carry out a role play centered on dealing with a difficult customer...

PRESENTATION

Common subjects include:

- Talk about yourself for 2 - 3 minutes
- Find out about another candidate, then present them to the group
- Talk about a subject you have some experience or interest in.

Deliver your talk in an upbeat way, without over-elaborating.

The recruiters are not so interested in the subject matter, they are more interested in how well candidates cope, and how comfortable they appear when addressing a group of people. They will also be looking for good delivery, and a certain amount of personal charisma.

For the self presentation, it is a good idea to practice a mini presentation in advance. By preparing for the self presentation in advance, you will gain the confidence you need.

During the mini presentation, introduce yourself to the group as well as the recruiters, share a few interesting personal facts and state why you want to be Cabin Crew.

Work on sounding natural, confident and friendly.

Below is a good example of a mini presentation

"Hi everyone, my name is Jane and it's really nice to meet you all. I'm 25 years old and live in the busy town of 'Any Town'. I currently work as a 'Freelance Hair Stylist'. It's a job I really enjoy because I have a lot of face to face contact with customers which is very important to me. One of the most rewarding aspects of my job is seeing the clients face glow with happiness when their hair is completely transformed. To know that I have made them happy makes me feel that I've done my job well.

I am looking for a change in career direction because being a member of Cabin Crew is something I have always wanted to do and I feel that the qualities I possess and the skills and experience I have gained through my work experience will make me an excellent member of Cabin Crew and a valuable asset to any airline.

Outside of work, I enjoy living life in the fast lane. Recently I did a 20 mile run for charity. I walked a lot of the way but was delighted to raise over £1,000 for Child line and become a little fitter in the process"

The example shows a highly positive and enthusiastic attitude right from the start. The greeting is personalised by greeting and addressing everyone. The focus is on the enjoyable parts of her work, her motives for making a change in career and her true personality outside of work.

FINAL NOTE

With each exercise, the airline is only narrowing the field by identifying the most suitable candidates. Therefore, teamwork starts here! Try to view your fellow candidates as future colleagues rather than rivals for a job.

The best advice I can offer when it comes to group activities is to 'expect anything and give it your all'.

Make your mini presentation enjoyable for others to listen to.

Use humour to assist you if you feel comfortable doing so (and providing its appropriate humour).

Ensure your tone of voice portrays your natural cheerful enthusiasm.

POSITIVE BEHAVIOUR DURING GROUP INTERVIEWS

- **Volunteer**
Always be one of the first few candidates to volunteer for anything. Volunteering is a great way to get the recruiters to notice you and also shows you are motivated, keen to get involved and are not afraid to take the initiative.

- **Make suggestions**
Making suggestions shows the recruiters that you are not afraid to express yourself and are keen to take part and get involved.

- **Maintain positive body language**
Most of your communication is done through your body language i.e. nodding, leaning slightly forward in your seat and overall showing a keenness to take part and get involved. If you are saying one thing but your body is showing another, the recruiters are likely to go with what your body is saying.

- **Speak loud and clear so that everyone can hear**
This point is self explanatory; if you are talking too quiet, it may be perceived as shy (not a cabin crew quality).

- **Be positive**
Remember that there is a good reason behind each element in the selection process - the recruiters are trying to find the right people for their airline. Be positive about the exercises and tests you are asked to undertake.

- **Use people's names where possible**
Using people's names is polite and shows certain level of respect. Most importantly, when the recruiters give their names, be sure to remember them.

- **Involve quieter members of the group**
If there are members of the team who are quite reserved, it is a good idea to get them involved by asking what they think or if they have any ideas. This shows empathy, a great quality for cabin crew.

- **Get involved in discussions but don't take over**

Those who cannot or will not get involved are not cabin crew material. For example: candidates who are too nervous, unable to put their point across, unwilling to commit, look bored, disinterested, aloof or bemused.

Equally, those who try to dominate or get over-involved are not suitable either. For example: Candidates who take control without seeking consensus, talk over or ignore the views of others, reject opinions because they do not agree with their own, or talk incessantly.

Teamwork and inter-personal skills are being investigated, so it is not primarily about leadership or even task completion. Good involvement is about achieving the right balance between expressing ones own opinions in a reasoned way, seeking consensus, and listening to/respecting the opinions of others.

- **Bring humour to the group**

If you feel comfortable and if it's appropriate humour, this will show the recruiters that you are comfortable being around new people and have a good sense of humour; it will also make the other candidates warm towards you which has many benefits.

- **Handling difficult situations**

Sometimes when you have a lot of different personalities in a group, a few of the candidates may take over the discussion, leaving other candidates unable to get a word in.

Should you encounter this situation, you will need to employ some strategies to get involved.

There are many ways you can ensure your involvement. You can sit forward, look directly at the person and with a smile, speak in a clear, firm, friendly tone of voice and say "I'm really sorry to have to interrupt you but I would really like to say something here" or if you really don't think you have the confidence to push your way in, you can simply raise your hand as you speak. Raising your hand will demand the attention of the group and let them know that you have something to say.

In either case, say what you want to say and then, still smiling, hand the conversation over to another member of the team "what do you think Mark?"

- **Remember to summarise**

  During a group task, there may come a point at which the ideas dry up and the discussion begins to go around in circles. The best thing to do in this situation is to summarise, 'so where have we got so far etc. Summarising gets the discussion past the awkward moments of silence and back on track.

- **Keep track of time**

  Good time keeping is crucial for working as cabin crew. If the recruiters give you a time limit for which to complete a particular task; this can be used to see who remains aware of the time limit and who does not. Keep your eye on the time and when you have a few minutes until the time is up, make the other candidates aware.

- **Don't be afraid to disagree**

  Disagreeing with others, if done in the right way can show that you are assertive yet considerate of others opinions.

  Consider the following example...

  In response to the topic "What 5 items would you as a group take to on an exploration trip to the moon?" a candidate suggests a pen knife. In response to this, you reply... "Yes - great idea! A knife is essential! How about we take a really multifunctional knife like a Swiss army knife?"

  This is positive behaviour. It leads with the word 'yes'. The original idea is embraced and supported. A new idea is introduced in a non-threatening way, by seeking consensus and using the pronoun "we".

  Selectors will be looking for positive behaviour such as this. Those who show negative behaviour will be rejected. Selectors will also be looking at non-verbal signals, such as body language and tone of voice, to ascertain that the observed behaviour is genuine.

IN A NUTSHELL

The most positive indicators for the cabin crew role are candidates who use humour to good effect, negotiate diplomatically, try to involve quieter group members, and go for team rather than individual solutions. Negative indicators are candidates who ignore or dismiss others, try to seize control, are selfish, aggressive, or purely task orientated.

So remember, get involved but don't try to take over. Be helpful and supportive to your fellow candidates - especially the quieter ones. Remember that the task is not really important, but the way you go about it is!

Group interviews can last from 9am to 5pm and may involve 2 or 3 sessions. In between each session, there will usually be a pause whilst selectors collate and consider their observations. After this some candidates may be sent home, leaving those who have proved most suitable to continue.

Along with the reasons outlined within the section 'What airlines look for', there is one prime reason why many candidates will be unsuccessful at a Cabin Crew interview.

The secret I am going to reveal to you now is the best kept secret within the airline industry.

When attending a Cabin Crew interview, candidates are focused on impressing the official recognised interviewers that make themselves known. This is all well and good but the truth is these are not the only interviewers...

As soon as you enter the interview venue, from the moment you walk through those doors, your interview has begun (if you are using the airline to travel to the venue, the working crew aboard the flight may be observing your behaviour which will then be reported back to the company). **Whether there is a small group of candidates or a large gathering, you are constantly being assessed, socially, personally and professionally.**

So, who are these other interviewers?

Well, you can never be sure about who the other interviewers are because they will take on various roles... they may be receptionists, janitors and even other fellow candidates... Yes, you did read that correct!

Airlines are aware that candidates will not necessarily show their true personalities to the recruiters themselves but will be much more natural with other candidates. Because of this, recruiters are in a much better position to find out what candidates are really like by going undercover as fellow candidates.

Undercover interviewers can take on a variety of different personalities. The personalities they choose can range from the one extreme of really shy and nervous or the other extreme of over-confident and/or back stabbing. Because of the many personalities they use, you can never be sure if the person is a genuine candidate or undercover interviewer. .

These interviewers are generally very good at their jobs and so the chances of you identifying them are low.

So how can you impress these interviewers if you don't know who to impress?

The answer to this question is very simple...

Treat everybody as though they are the interviewers. Don't show or tell anyone, anything, you wouldn't want to show or say to the recruiters themselves.

So, demonstrate a positive attitude, appear friendly and relaxed and be helpful and supportive to other candidates.

Leaving the venue

Don't let yourself assume that because the interview has finished you can relax... NO... Leaving the venue, whether successful or not, is still a very crucial moment that can affect your chances of being offered a position either now or in the future.

When you leave the venue, you will likely be departing along with other candidates and therefore, undercover interviewers...

FINAL NOTE

Undercover interviewers can fail or pass the interview just like genuine candidates.

The reasons why an interviewer will fail is because most candidates will show their true personalities when they think they have failed. Airlines, especially Virgin are aware that many candidates will return after 6 months to try again and this is the ideal opportunity to find out if these candidates are worthy of a second interview.

Likewise, interviewers can also pass the group stage. In fact, interviewers can be the only ones who are successful. The ones that pass do so because they have provided genuine candidates with a good example of the kind of qualities the airline is seeking in their potential cabin crew.

The fact is that these undercover interviewers are the reason why 90% of candidates fail at the group stage and it is therefore very important that no matter how confident you feel that another candidate is genuine, you must treat everyone as if they are your interviewers.

Even if you don't encounter an undercover interviewer, you will still be assessed on how you treat fellow candidates.

Aptitude Tests

When carrying out any kind of aptitude test, it is important that you read the questions through fully and make sure you completely understand what is being asked before attempting to answer.

I would suggest that you begin by going through the test sheet and complete all the questions you find easy first and leave the ones that you find tricky to return back to later. This way, you can be confident that you have answered as many questions as possible.

It is also a good idea to go through a final check when you are finished to ensure that no mistakes have been made. Due to this, I would highly recommend that you mark your answers in pencil at first so that when you are completing your final check, any mistakes can be easily rectified.

MATHS

Many maths questions will allow you to use a calculator but the recruitment team won't normally allow you to use a calculator to work out the basic maths questions. To be on the safe side, it is a good idea to brush up on some of the basics which I have outlined below.

In order to not insult your intelligence, I am going to presume during this short instruction that you are already aware of units, 10's, 100's etc... and how to add and subtract.

MULTIPLICATION
Short Multiplication

Short multiplication is when the multiplying number is less than 10.
E.g. 165 x 7.

Units: 7 x 5 = 35, which is 5 carry 3
Tens: 7 x 6 = 42 + carried 3 = 45, which is 5 carry 4
Hundreds: 7 x 1 = 7 + carried 4 = 11, which is 1 carry 1
There are no more digits to be multiplied by 7, the carried 1 becomes 1 thousand

Your working out should look something like this:

$$x\begin{array}{r}165 \\ 7 \\ \hline 1155 \end{array}$$

Multiplying a whole number by 10, 100, 1000...

10 – The units become 10's, the 10's become 100's, 100's become 1000's etc...
100 – The units become 100's, the 10's become 1000's etc...
1000 – The units become 1000's, the 10's become 10000's etc...

For example...　　753 x 10 = 7530
　　　　　　　　　753 x 100 = 75300
　　　　　　　　　753 x 1000 = 753000

Multiplying whole numbers by multiples of 10 (20, 30, 40...)

Multiplying by 40 is the same as multiplying by 10 and then multiplying by 4.

20 – 753 x 10 x 2
30 – 753 x 10 x 3
40 – 753 x 10 x 4

Long Multiplication

Long multiplication is used when the multiplying number is greater than 10

E.g. 24 x 17

A standard non calculator method for doing long multiplication multiplies the number by:

The units figure, then
The tens figure, then
The hundreds figure, and so on
All these answers are added together...

To work out 24 x 17

```
   24
x  17
  168  ➡ 24 x 7
  240  ➡ 24 x 10
  408
```

Multiplying Decimals

2.53

Whole   Decimal Part
Number   (5 tenths
         3 hundreds)

Multiplying decimals by the power of:
10 – Each figure moves 1 place to the left
100 – Each figure moves 2 places to the left
1000 – Each figure moves 3 places to the left

E.g.

2.76
27.6   - 2.76 x 10
276.   - 2.76 x 100
2760.   - 2.76 x 1000

1   Ignore the decimal points and multiply the numbers using long multiplication
2   Count the total number of decimal places in the numbers being multiplied
    together
3   Place the decimal point so that the answer has the same total number of
    decimal places

E.g.

4.25
x 0.18
3400 → 425 x 8
4250 → 425 x 10
0.7650 → The answer must have 4 decimal places
         because 4.25 and 0.18 has 2 decimal places

DIVISION
Short Division

The process of dividing a number by a number less than 10 is called short division.

Division is the opposite operation to multiplication...

If $A \div B = C$
Then $C \times B = A$

To work out $882 \div 7$, we would set our working out like this: $7\overline{)882}$ or $7\underline{)882}$

Starting from the left:

$8 \div 7 = 1$ remainder 1 (which is 1 carry 1)
$18 \div 7 = 2$ remainder 4 (2 carry 4)
$42 \div 7 = 6$ with no remainder

So $882 \div 7 = 126$

Your working out should look something like this:

```
    Remainders
      /^
7 | 8 8 2
    1 2 6
          \Answer
```

You can check your division by multiplying.

Does $126 \times 7 = 882$?

Dividing a whole number by 10, 100, 1000...

When you divide a whole number by:

10 – The 10's become units, the 100's become 10's, 1000's become 100's etc...
100 – The 100's become units, the 1000's become 10's etc...
1000 – The 1000's become units, the 10,000's become 10's etc...

For example... $7530 \div 10 = 753$
$12\,400 \div 100 = 124$
$631\,000 \div 1000 = 631$

Dividing a whole number by multiples of 10 (20, 30, 40…)

Consider: $7530 \div 30$

Dividing by 30 is the same as dividing by 10 and then dividing by 3.

$7530 \div 10 = 753$
$753 \div 3 = 251$

Long Division

Long division works in exactly the same way as short division except all the working out is written down.

Long division process…

÷ (Obtain biggest answer possible)

x
 } Calculates
- } the remainder

Bring down the next figure

Repeat the process until there are no more figures to be brought down.

Consider: $952 \div 7$

```
    136
7 ) 952
    7
    25
    21
    42
    42
     0
```

$9 \div 7 = 1$ and a remainder
What is the remainder?
$1 \times 7 = 7$ (write below the 9)
$9 - 7 = 2$ (which is the remainder)
Bring down the next figure (5) to make 25
Repeat the above process
$25 \div 7 = 3$ and a remainder
$3 \times 7 = 21$, $25 - 21 = 4$ (remainder)
Bring down the next figure (2) to make 42
And repeat the process
$42 \div 7 = 6$ but there is no remainder
$6 \times 7 = 42$, $42 - 42 = 0$ (remainder)
There are no more figures to be brought down and there is no remainder
So $952 \div 7 = 136$

Dividing Decimals

To divide by a decimal:
1. Multiply the dividing number by the power of 10 (10, 100, 1000…) so that it becomes a whole number.
2. Multiply the number to be divided by the same number.
3. If necessary the answer will have a decimal point in the same place.

Work out $2.4 \div 0.4$

$$\frac{2.4}{0.4} = \frac{2.4 \times 10}{0.4 \times 10} = \frac{24}{4} = 6$$

FOREIGN CURRENCY

The good news with currency conversion is that you will normally be allowed to use a calculator. Following is a simple method on how to carry out conversions from and to foreign currencies…

To exchange GB Pounds (local currency) into Euros (foreign currency)…
Multiply the foreign rate of exchange by the total number of Pound Sterling
For example…   Total price to be exchanged = £200 GBP
               1.55 Euros = £1 GBP
               1.55 Euros x 200 = 310 Euros

To exchange Malaysian Ringgits (foreign) into US Dollars (local)…
Divide the total number of foreign currency by the rate of exchange

For example…   Total price to be exchanged = 300 Ringgits
               8 Ringgits = USD $1
               300 Ringgits ÷ 8 = USD $37.50

PSYCHOMETRIC

Many airlines believe that psychometric tests provide a clear assessment of a candidate's ability to carry out a job, and whether the character of an individual will complement the current working environment.

If survey statistics are to be believed, up to 56% of candidates exaggerate their skills/experience on their resume. Therefore making a recruitment decision purely on the content of a resume could prove to be unreliable and whilst a resume certainly provides an overview of a candidate's ability and work experience, it doesn't necessarily illustrate how they may work within certain circumstances.

Likewise, an applicant may handle an interview extremely well but not have the capability to deliver the role itself, or vice versa.

Psychometric testing helps to build a profile of characteristics, behavioural style and personality. For example, how does a candidate interact with others? How do they react within a certain situation? Is a candidate able to do the job for which they have applied? Is a candidate a natural leader with individual initiative? Etc...

When psychometric testing is used during the recruitment process, the airline has, or should have, a clear idea of the sort of person they are looking to recruit. If you are not that sort of person, then you are unlikely to be happy in the job in the long term, no matter how superficially attractive it may be.

Consequently, candidates try to imagine how the employer wants them to be and then answer the questions in such a way as to give a favourable impression. This is doomed to failure for the following reason.

Many psychometric tests have in-built checking mechanisms (built in lie detectors) for detecting individuals who are attempting to create an overly favourable impression. Many tests also include questions that check if you are telling the truth!

My heart felt advice is to answer the questions as honestly as possible.

Following is a basic example of how a psychometric assessment is generally carried out and the types of questions you may be asked...

Mark each of the following statements on a scale of 1 to 5 where:
1 = Strongly agree   2 = Agree   3 = Not sure   4 = Disagree   5 = Strongly disagree

Score

1	**At work, I like to be told exactly what to do**	1	2	3	4	5
2	If you want something done properly, you have to do it yourself	1	2	3	4	5
3	We often need help and advice from our superiors	1	2	3	4	5
4	I find it easy to relax after a hard day	1	2	3	4	5
5	I would like to win the lottery and retire early	1	2	3	4	5
6	Most people are honest	1	2	3	4	5
7	I have a career development plan in mind	1	2	3	4	5
8	I believe that the end justifies the means	1	2	3	4	5
9	Would you prefer to be an author (1) or an actor (2)	1	2	?		
10	I can achieve anything if I try hard enough	1	2	3	4	5
11	I enjoy meeting new people	1	2	3	4	5
12	I get bored doing repetitive tasks	1	2	3	4	5
13	I often lose my temper when I am frustrated	1	2	3	4	5
14	Who do you admire more – Madonna (1) or Mahatma Gandhi (2)	1	2	?		
15	I need alcohol to give me confidence around other people	1	2	3	4	5
16	I prefer working independently rather than in a team	1	2	3	4	5
17	I fall sick often	1	2	3	4	5
18	I always think before I act	1	2	3	4	5
19	I respect my superiors decisions even if I don't agree	1	2	3	4	5
20	I knew what career I wanted when I left school	1	2	3	4	5
21	Worrying keeps me awake at night	1	2	3	4	5
22	I am often lost for words when meeting people for the first time	1	2	3	4	5
23	I feel dissatisfied with my career progress to date	1	2	3	4	5
24	Are you more introvert (1) or extrovert (2)	1	2	?		
25	I often feel overwhelmed	1	2	3	4	5
26	I enjoy challenges	1	2	3	4	5
27	I make mistakes when I rush	1	2	3	4	5
28	I have an active social life	1	2	3	4	5
29	I sometimes feel depressed with my life	1	2	3	4	5
30	Do you prefer using the stairs (1) or an escalator (2)	1	2	?		
31	I feel confident about my future	1	2	3	4	5
32	I plan activities rather than just going ahead and doing it	1	2	3	4	5
33	I can't work with people I don't like	1	2	3	4	5

34	I listen politely to people with whom I deeply disagree	1	2	3	4	5
35	I find it difficult to bounce back after disappointment	1	2	3	4	5
36	Do you prefer to work with your hands (1) or your brain (2)	1	2	?		
37	I value my reputation for straight talking	1	2	3	4	5
38	When I worry, I bottle it up inside	1	2	3	4	5
39	I need others to motivate me	1	2	3	4	5
40	I can work on my own initiative	1	2	3	4	5
41	I am easily stressed	1	2	3	4	5
42	Are you more productive in the morning (1) or in the evening (2)	1	2	?		
43	I would make a good salesperson	1	2	3	4	5
44	I tire easily	1	2	3	4	5
45	I stand up for what I believe	1	2	3	4	5
46	I sometimes cut corners to get a job done quicker	1	2	3	4	5
47	I would like to be somebody else	1	2	3	4	5
48	Would you rather sit and read a book (1) or go for a walk (2)	1	2	?		
49	I sometimes lie to get what I want	1	2	3	4	5
50	I am a good leader	1	2	3	4	5
51	I take criticism personally	1	2	3	4	5
52	I am a fast learner	1	2	3	4	5
53	Is it more important to be truthful (1) or tactful (2)	1	2	?		
54	I feel most relaxed in my own company	1	2	3	4	5
55	Do you prefer to talk (1) or listen (2)	1	2	?		
56	I remain calm under pressure	1	2	3	4	5
57	I am often late arriving at work	1	2	3	4	5
58	People respect my opinions	1	2	3	4	5
59	I would leave work immediately if a family member became ill	1	2	3	4	5
60	I am confident when addressing a group	1	2	3	4	5

LANGUAGE

If a second language is a requirement of the airline or if English isn't your native language, you may be required to carry out a language assessment.

If a language assessment is required, you could be assessed for the four key skills:

- listening
- speaking
- reading
- writing

These skills can be assessed within three modes of communication:

- interpersonal (involving two-way interactive communication)
- interpretive (relating to the understanding of spoken or written language) and
- presentational (involving creating spoken or written communication)

Communicative ability may be assessed through authentic communication tasks as called for in daily working life on board an aircraft.

Performances on assessment tasks will be evaluated by how well the candidate understands (comprehension) and can be understood (comprehensibility). The evaluation considers language knowledge, the appropriate use of communication strategies, and the application of cultural knowledge to enhance communication.

GENERAL KNOWLEDGE

You may be required to complete a general knowledge test.

It is therefore advisable to brush up on your general knowledge and familiarity with capital cities/currencies/time zones of the world, airline codes, airport codes and current affairs.

> Rather than learning every world currency, time zone, airline code etc... Try to focus on becoming familiar with the major countries/cities/airlines.

Below is a basic example of a general knowledge test sheet which includes the kinds of questions you may be asked.

1   Emirates Airlines has its own 2 digit airline code prefix, what is it?
2   How many European countries are members of the EU?
3   How many cigarettes can you bring back from a non-EU to an EU country?
4   In relation to time, what do the letters GMT stand for?
5   Which airline bears the letters AA?
6   What is the currency of Thailand?
7   What are to two major models of aircraft carriers that the airline industry use?
8   Which major airline in the UK sports a red Cabin Crew uniform?
9   It is 1100 hours British summertime in the UK, what is the time in New York?
10 What is the name of the highest mountain in the world?
11 Which is the busiest airport in the world?
12 What do the letters ATC stand for?
13 What is the capital of Australia?
14 What is the airport code for London Heathrow?
15 In which country would you find the River Nile?
16 What is the name of the new European Double Decker Jumbo Jet Aircraft?
17 Where on an aircraft would you find a hat rack?
18 Which is the biggest country in the world?
19 Which country has the largest population?
20 In which country would you find the 'Rupee' currency?
21 What is the time zone of Tokyo?
22 Which is the smallest country in the world?
23 What is the currency of Europe?
24 Which languages are spoken in Canada?

At some point during the selection process, you may be required to be measured against the airlines criteria.

Airlines can be very strict when it comes to height and weight proportions so you must ensure that you meet the airlines specific requirements and that the information you have given regarding you measurements are correct. If incorrect, it is likely that they will terminate your interview at this stage.

Airlines generally only require that your weight is in proportion to your height and that you don't fall below the minimum or exceed their maximum height.

- **Height**

  The height restrictions vary from airline to airline, however a typical minimum height is 5 foot 2 inches (158 cms) and a typical maximum is 6 foot 2 inches (188 cms).

  There may be a lower height restriction at some bases where the aircraft type operated has a maximum height allowance of 5 foot 10 inches

- **Weight**

  The Body Mass Index (BMI) is a formula used by health professionals throughout the world to assess an adult's body weight in relation to their height. Following is a BMI chart for you to work out your own proportions.

  Please note: *if the majority of your body mass is made up of muscle, if you are pregnant or lactating, you should not use this chart as a guide.*

Find your height and read down the column until you find the weight nearest to yours, then read across for the appropriate BMI...

Height (Inches/Metres)

60(1.5)	62(1.55)	64(1.6)	66(1.65)	68(1.7)	70(1.75)	72(1.8)	74(1.85	BMI
Weight (lb/kg)								
89(40)	95(43)	101(46)	108(49)	115(52)	121(55)	128(58)	135(61)	18
94(43)	100(45)	107(49)	114(52)	121(55)	128(58)	135(61)	143(65)	19
99(45)	105(48)	113(51)	120(54)	127(58)	135(61)	143(65)	150(68)	20
104(47)	111(50)	118(54)	126(57)	134(61)	141(64)	150(68)	158(72)	21
109(49)	116(53)	124(56)	132(60)	140(64)	148(67)	157(71)	166(75)	22
114(52)	121(55)	130(59)	138(63)	146(66)	155(70)	164(74)	173(78)	23
119(54)	127(58)	135(61)	144(65)	153(69)	162(73)	171(78)	181(82)	24
124(56)	132(60)	141(64)	150(68)	159(72)	168(76)	178(81)	188(85)	25
139(63)	148(67)	158(72)	167(76)	178(81)	188(85)	200(91)	210(95)	28
148(67)	158(72)	169(77)	180(82)	191(87)	202(92)	214(97)	226(103)	30
173(78)	185(84)	197(90)	210(95)	222(101)	236(107)	250(113)	263(119)	35
198(90)	211(96)	225(102)	240(109)	254(115)	270(122)	260(118)	301(137)	40

BMI UNDER 18.5 *Classification: Underweight*
BMI 18.5 - 24.99 *Classification: Normal range*
BMI 25 - 29.99 *Classification: Overweight (Pre Obese)*
BMI 30 - 34.99 *Classification: Obese Class 1*
BMI 35 - 40 *Classification: Obese Class 2*
BMI OVER 40 *Classification: Obese Class 3 (Extreme Obesity)*

If your own height or weight isn't on the chart, then you can use the following formula to calculate your own BMI.

The calculation is simple: BMI = your weight in kilograms divided by your height in metres squared...
- To get your weight in kilograms, divide your weight in pounds by 2.2
- To get your height in metres, multiply your height in inches by 0.025
- Squared height is your height multiplied by itself (e.g. 1.65 x 1.65 = 2.72)

So for someone who is 53kg in weight with a height of 2.72m ^{2}, we would calculate the following...
53 ÷ 2.72 = 19.48
So this persons BMI is 19.48 which puts them in the classification of normal range.

If you have reached this point of the selection process – *Congratulations...* The recruitment team clearly likes what they have seen and now all that is needed is further clarification that you have the qualities, skills and experience they are looking for.

> **Be Prepared**
> Your interview may consist of a group or single applicant meeting with a panel or a two on one interview

DO

- **Keep your mind focused on the interview**
  If you are thinking about how you look, what you are going to say next or have you failed, etc then you most likely will fail. You need to be completely focused on what the recruiters are saying in order to be able to give the best possible answers.

- **Listen to the entire question before responding**
  This if for two reasons; first, you may think that you know the answer before the interviewer finishes asking the question but you may be surprised and find that the interviewer was going to ask a different question to that which you assumed. Second, if you interrupt the interviewer whilst they are asking a question, it will come across as very disrespectful. Be patient and you will get time to give your answer in due course.

- **Make sure you understand the question before attempting to answer it**
  It is better to ask the interviewer to repeat the question than to try to answer it without completely understanding or hearing it. If you give an answer to a question that wasn't asked, it looks unprofessional and will give the impression that you are not listening.

- **Give detailed yet concise answers and check that the interview would like you to continue**
  If an answer is too long winded, the interviewer will become complacent. Try to reveal as much information as you can with the least amount of words as possible (this is where preparation comes in handy) - The answers provided in this book will help you achieve this.

- **Speak slight slower than normal**
  This will ensure that the recruiters completely understand what you are saying and also stop you from falling over your words.

- **Vary the tone of your voice to add interest**
  When the tone of your voice varies, it makes what you are saying more interesting. If your voice is monotone, it may be perceived as though you are not enthusiastic. It can also make the recruiters not want to listen.

- **Put emotional meaning into what you are saying**
  By doing this simple thing, you will sound and come across as genuine and will also keep the recruiters interested in what you are saying.

- **Maintain open gestures**
  Maintaining open gestures makes you come across as sincere, confident and honest. Crossing your arms is a closed posture and makes you appear nervous and dishonest.

- **Indicate that you are listening and interested in what the recruiters are saying**
  You can do this by nodding, leaning slightly forward in your seat and occasionally saying yes, ok, etc.

- **Maintain eye contact**
  Maintain eye contact with the person who asks you the question; however do occasionally engage eye contact with the 2nd interviewer (If direct eye contact is too much, look at the bridge of the nose).. By doing this simple thing, your first impression is one of somebody who is confident.

- **Speak clearly, open your mouth wide enough to talk properly**
  Sometimes when we are nervous, we don't open our mouths widely enough to talk properly. When this happens, it comes across to other people as mumbling.

- **Project professionalism**
  When we are feeling nervous or panicky, we tend to use more gestures and adopt habits like touching the hair and face, nail biting, foot tapping, fidgeting etc…

  Minimum movement suggests that you are in control and calm. So, in order to be perceived as professional and calm, try to control any nervous habits you may have - even if it means sitting on your hands…

- **Remember that you are interviewing them too**
  You are interviewing the recruiters as much as they are interviewing you. Is this the airline you want to work for? Does the airline have the kind of values and environment you would be happy working in?

- **Remember to Smile**
  As cabin crew, you will be dealing with all kinds of people and pressures every day, so a genuine and sincere looking smile is one of the must have qualities. If you can't fake it, just think about how lucky the recruiters are to be meeting you.

- **Use mirroring techniques**
  Mirroring techniques happen naturally when you have developed a rapport with another person, your body subconsciously and subtly copy the movements and gestures of the other person. By using mirroring techniques, you will establish a rapport with the interviewer, but don't be obvious.

DON'T

- **Don't panic when your mind goes blank**
  If your mind goes blank, don't say the first thing that comes into your head. Breathe deeply and play for time by saying something like 'that's an interesting question', this will give you time to collect your thoughts,

- **Don't worry about nerves**
  They never show to other people as much as you think they do. Worrying about them will make you more nervous, THINK POSITIVE.

- **Don't worry about silence**
  Silence in a job interview can be either your powerful ally or your worst enemy. When you talk to the interviewer or answer his/her questions, use pauses to emphasize your point and to build up eager anticipation for what you are going to say next.

Those periods of silence will give you an opportunity to make eye contact with the interviewer and study his reactions to what you've just said. Don't hesitate to use silence. Speak in a slow, relaxed manner. Pause every now and then to grab the interviewer's attention.

Some recruiters use silence as a tool for eliciting further response from a candidate. Once you say what you wanted to say, they will leave you in limbo for a few, very long seconds. You must resist the urge to say something just to break that silence.

- **Avoid using too many um's and ah's etc...**
  As much as possible, refrain from interjecting your comments with uhs, you knows, ums and the like. It's no sin to pause and say nothing while gathering your thoughts.

- **Don't shake hands with sweaty palms**
  If this is something you have a problem with, try using talcum powder and keep a hanky close to hand.

- **Don't be negative**
  This is a big no no; be especially careful about being negative about other jobs, airlines, people, previous employers and your current job.

- **Avoid using phrases such as 'I don't know', 'I disagree', 'why do you want to know that?' etc...**
  If you can avoid saying any of these things, it would be beneficial as they are negative phrases, however, if there really is a need to tell them you don't know something etc there are ways of saying these things without them sounding negative.

- **Don't worry about there being more than one interviewer**
  Believe it or not, it is easy to deal with more than one interviewer. When there is just the one, you have to maintain constant eye contact throughout the interview with that one person. When there is a second interviewer, you can break eye contact and look at the recruiters in turn which makes maintaining eye contact a whole lot easier.

- **Don't take negative questions personally**
  Sometimes, recruiters will ask a series of negative questions such as 'How would you react if I told you that your presentation this afternoon was lousy?' or 'How would you respond if I told you that your skills/experience were below the requirements of this position?' Don't take these types of questions personally as the recruiters are asking them to get a reaction from you. Your reaction should be a positive one that reinforces the reasons why the airline should hire you.

- **Don't smoke**
  Even if it is allowed, don't smoke during the interview process. Many airlines will not consider applicants who smoke due to the non-smoking environments you will be working in. Also, the smell of smoke will linger on your clothing which can be unpleasant.

Leave a positive lasting impression

During the first few minutes of the interview, the interviewer makes certain judgments about your character and work style based on your dress, demeanour and body language.

Following is a good example of how to deal with those first and last crucial moments...

Introduction.
Offer hand to shake. "Jane Doe; it's nice to meet you." (Smile)

Would you like something to drink?
If drinks are in the room already, then say "yes please" and have one if you want. **Avoid biscuits!!!**

If drinks are not in the room, say "if you are having one, I'll join you, but otherwise I'm fine, thank you".

How was your journey?
No problems. Your map was a great help.

Departing the interview room with etiquette.
Gather belongings and ensure you have a tight grip on them.

Stand up and straighten your clothes. Shake hands with your interviewer(s) if this is expected (when shaking hands, simply say "thank you for giving me the opportunity to meet with you, I look forward to hearing from you.") and Smile.

Make your exit by – stopping at the door – turning, smiling and thanking again – leave, closing the door quietly behind you.

Part 2a

Part 2a

Questions & Answers

In this part...

Cabin crew interview questions are fairly unique in that the questioning tends to focus almost exclusively on personal qualities. As a result, there are no definite right or wrong answers, just more appropriate answers and better forms of expression.

It is important to have examples ready, to back up any statements made. For example "I enjoy providing customer care" may be investigated with the follow up: "When have you provided good customer care?" or perhaps a statement like "I appreciate there are times when a crew member has to remain calm under pressure" would be followed with the question "When have you experienced a pressured situation?"

In the following pages, I have listed various interview questions, followed by examples of effective ways to answering each of them in a detailed, yet concise manner (examples of follow up questions are also provided where necessary to give you an idea of what to expect). Whilst the answers provided are based around an individual whose career is in hairdressing, each of the answers may be adapted to suit your individual circumstance.

Please remember...

The answers provided on the following pages are designed to be used as a guide to assist you in formulating your own answers and should not be copied in their entirety.

Create
Guidelines for creating
your own answers

When a question that is asked is based around a personal experience you have encountered, try to keep to the following guidelines when formulating your answers...

- Choose an experience that demonstrates an interaction that resulted in a positive experience for all concerned
- Try to keep your answers detailed yet concise
- Begin by briefly stating what happened
- Go on to describe what you did and how you dealt with the situation
- Briefly describe your feelings and concerns when you were faced with the situation and how the other person may have also felt
- Describe the outcome
- Explain how your actions affected the other person/outcome
- Then state what you learned from the experience

Below is a good example of an answer which covers each of these points...

What happened?

"I recently experienced a situation with a client who was having relationship problems and who became very emotional."

How the client may have felt

"I could sense that she was feeling very depressed and I tried to think of what I could do to help. "

What I did

"I gave her chance to talk while I listened. This seemed to calm her down. Once I heard her story, I showed empathy and concern for her situation whilst not getting too involved. "

How I felt

"It was a difficult situation and I felt compassion for the client's situation. It was a real struggle to maintain my poised mask, but I managed to keep my emotions under control."

Positive outcome and how my actions affected the client/outcome

"As a result of my listening and showing concern, the client began seeing her situation more clearly and became much more positive. Consequently, she was able to calmly discuss her feelings with her partner and work through their problems. She later thanked me for listening and told me I was very caring. It made me feel good that I was able to make such a big difference. She's now a regular client of mine."

What I learned from this experience

"From this experience, I learned that just listening can be providing good customer care and ultimately change someone's future to a more positive one."

Do your best have several positive experiences prepared before the interview and make sure the experiences are true.

Questions & Answers
Contents

These kinds of questions draw from personal experience, and are fairly easy to answer, so they are often used to settle candidates into an interview. Selectors also use background questions as a reference point from which to introduce the more role-specific questions.

> Be positive about the work you do and about your outside interests. Negative and pessimistic attitudes are unlikely to advance your cause! Also, if you consider the kind of qualities selectors are trying to identify, you will be better able to phrase your replies to make the most favourable impression.

Recruiters are likely to probe with follow up questions if they think there are revealing aspects about qualities they wish to explore (or potential problems, such as long/frequent periods of sickness).

PERSONAL DETAILS

How would the job impact your family/home life?
The impact would not be great, if any as I can keep in contact easily through the internet and using the telephone.

What do your family think about you applying for this position/your chosen career?
My family understand the decision I have made and support me 100%.

This position requires long hours, will this be a problem for your family life?
My career plays an important part of my life. My family and friends realise and appreciate the fact and are very flexible with my schedule. They support me 100 percent.

OUTSIDE INTERESTS

What do you do to relax after a hard day?
After a hard day, I either go for a swim, a sauna or perform my yoga and relaxation routines to make a break from the environment and help me unwind.

What is your energy level like/Where do you get your energy from?
My energy levels are on top form; working freelance isn't possible unless you have plenty of energy. To keep them that way; I routinely involve myself in cardiovascular exercise. If you have too much energy, cardiovascular exercise uses some of it up. If I have too little it stimulates the body's systems and finds you some.

Your interests appear rather solitary, cycling, swimming, running, reading, yoga etc. How do you think this reflects your personality?
I like to think they suggest a sense of balance. In my work I spend a lot of time with clients and I have an active social life outside of work, so it can be good to relax sometimes and do something completely different. In any case, these activities, I quite often do with company.

What have you achieved through your interests?
Apart from the obvious benefits, such as fitness and stamina, I have achieved a healthier, stress free lifestyle. My interests have also helped me develop my team spirit and ability to work with others towards a common goal.

EDUCATION AND TRAINING
School

Why didn't you do better in your exams?
My results were above average, as with most other people, if I could do it again, my grades would be much higher. I'd not only work harder, but I've also learned a lot since then.

What were your favourite subjects?
I always felt great interest towards Geography; I am fascinated by the changing world. I particularly enjoyed learning about different continents – terrains, cultures, the environments, the landscapes etc...

What subjects gave you the most difficulty?
I never had a great deal of knowledge about science, but I forced myself to study hard so I managed to achieve above average results.

What subjects were the easiest for you?
I wouldn't say that any of the subjects were easy, as they all required hard work. However, because I have a natural creative ability, Art and Design was the one I found to be the least difficult. I felt a great deal of pleasure from those lessons and my exam results were outstanding.

I see you studied French at school, what is your fluency?
I studied French in high school and found the language very interesting. I am not as fluent as I once was, I understand a lot of the basics, such as greetings, introducing myself, the alphabet and numbers 1 -100 etc. I would welcome the opportunity to increase my fluency.

Why didn't you stay on at school or continue full time education/ Do you feel you made the right choice?
I did consider continuing full time education, but I had really enjoyed my work experience at Any Hair Salon, and wanted to start on work I enjoyed as soon as possible, it wasn't long before I realised I had made the right choice.

Or

I wanted to continue full time education, but personal circumstances meant that I needed to earn a living rather than run up debts studying. Education comes from places other than college.

Further Education and Training

Tell us about your further education and training/What steps have you taken to increase your skills and experience?
Since leaving school I have used every opportunity to expand my knowledge and acquire further skills. Whilst working at Any Hair Salon, I studied part time to achieve my NVQ levels 1, 2 and 3 in hairdressing. During this time, I also completed a creative cutting course, alongside the comprehensive on-the-job training I received through the salon,

I also educate myself informally through reading journals and reviewing self help techniques in books; and I subscribe to trade magazines. So I have continued to learn and grow.

What areas of self development do you study through books?
Delivering customer care, dealing with difficult situations/complaints, stress management, etc.

What do you do to improve yourself?
I don't think a day has passed in my career that I didn't improve my skills to some extent. I've always found that if you want to learn, there's plenty to be picked up every day.

As a hairstylist the learning and development process never ends. Not only are you developing your practical skills but also your social skills.

General

Do you feel you're education and training prepared you well for the challenges in the work force?
My education and training gave me a solid foundation on which I built my knowledge base and gave me the confidence to face the future challenges. To achieve good results at school I had to work hard, set my goals and do my best to achieve them. The same principles apply in the work force. The problem-solving and goal-setting skills that I acquired have helped me a lot throughout my career.

How has your education prepared you for the role of Cabin Crew?
This position requires knowledge and skills that I acquired through my education and training, such as dealing with customers, working as part of a team and selling products/services. Many of the subjects I studied at school are also directly related to the job such as English, Geography and Mathematics, yet what school really taught me that has helped throughout my career and will prove very useful to this position was how to solve problems, how to apply myself, and how to set a goal and achieve it.

Do you think grades should be considered by new employers?
Of course, an employer should take everything into consideration, and along with grades will be an evaluation of willingness and manageability, an understanding of how business works, and actual work experience. Combined, such experience and professional skills can be more valuable than grades alone.

What is your opinion of the importance of training and development?
Effective training and development is absolutely necessary in order to improve efficiency and readiness for the work force.

I see you are currently learning Spanish, what is your level of fluency/How long have you been learning it?

As the language is very similar to French, I am picking it up fairly quickly, however, I have only recently begun learning the language. Hopefully, in the next few months I should gain a basic level of reading, writing and speaking.

WORK EXPERIENCE AND EMPLOYMENT HISTORY
Previous Employers

How would you evaluate any hair salon /Was it a good salon to work for/ What did you like about the environment?

I can say only good things about Any Hair Salon. There was always a vibrant atmosphere, the people were great – they were very talented and fantastically professional. There were no arbitrary lines between seniority and staff, but rather a team of skilled professionals all working together. I was given all the opportunities that were available and received more hands on training and attention than I could ever have hoped for.

Why did you choose to work at Any Hair Salon?

Initially, I chose Any Hair Salon because of the familiarity after having carried out two weeks of work experience within the salon whilst I was at school. However, I also chose the salon in particular because of its good reputation and practicality and having been a customer on several occasions, I knew it was the salon I wanted to work for. The salon had an atmosphere all of its own and it wasn't long before I realised I had made the right choice.

What reputation did the salon have/what had you heard about the salon?

They had a reputation for being a very likeable place - Great service, talented workers, good customer care, and vibrant atmosphere.

What did you wish you knew about the salon before you started?
I had done work experience within the salon and had also been a customer on more than one occasion, because of this, everything that I wanted or needed to know, I already knew.

What could Any Hair Salon have done better?
As an employer, they were fine and I have no complaints. As for the service and customer care, I don't think we could have done better. There was always a vibrant atmosphere, the people were great – they were very talented and fantastically professional.

If probed further
I really can't think of anything that could have been improved. Anything that could have been improved had already been done.

Or

Any Hair Salon never gave me anything to complain about. I knew that it was a wonderful salon.

Why did you stay with the same employer for so long?
I was there for several years, but in a variety of different roles so it felt as though I was undergoing frequent changes without actually changing employer.

Co-workers

Tell us about your last work group/Did you get along with your co workers?
My colleagues at Any Hair Salon were good natured but serious about work. There were only 8 of us in the team upon leaving (including myself and the manager), which made for a very relaxed atmosphere. We all became close and worked well as a team. I enjoyed the time I spent with them.

Did being close cause problems during work?
No, there were no problems. We worked very professionally together.

How DO superiors get the best out of you?
My superiors always got superior effort and performance, but by treating me like a human being and giving me the same personal respect with which they liked to be treated themselves was definitely an added motivator.

What did you dislike about your superiors? How could your superiors have done a better job?
You know, I've never thought of our relationship in terms of like or dislike. I've always thought our role was to get along together and get the job done. I have always had the highest respect for my superiors and they couldn't have done a better job.

Surely there must have been something you disliked about them!
I'm lucky to have had very supportive superiors who were good at their jobs and very easy to work with. I honestly can't think of anything that I disliked or could have been improved.

(No matter how much the recruiters probe, don't be drawn into divulging criticism – stick to your guns)

Present Employment

What do you like about your current job?
I like everything about my current job. I don't think I'd be able to really excel if I weren't truly interested in the work, or if I were merely motivated by its financial rewards.

Rather than pick out little details of the routine work, here are three general things. First, customer satisfaction, seeing the clients face glow with happiness when their hair has been transformed, it's very satisfying and drives me to do better. Second, I like constant interaction with people; it has enabled me to strengthen my communication and customer care skills.

And finally, I enjoy being creative with hair, and finding new ways to please the customer.

What have you enjoyed most about working freelance/your current job?

I enjoy the freedom, identity and status. I have the freedom to set my own goals and work to my own schedule. I have control over the products I use and can plan and use my time more effectively. I also enjoy the feeling of pride when I say goodbye to another satisfied client.

> **If you get this job, you will not have the freedom to work to your own schedule, is this going to be a problem?**
> No, this will not be a problem as my current job requires me to be very flexible. So if I was to get this job, I would naturally adapt.

What particular aspect of your job do you find most rewarding/What is your favourite part of the job?

The most rewarding aspect of my job is definitely seeing the clients face glow with happiness when their hair has been transformed, it's very satisfying and makes me proud to see what I have done.

What do you dislike about your current job/What is the worst part of the job?

I really like this work, so I honestly can't think of any major dislikes. I guess my answer will have to come under the category or nuisances. The biggest nuisance is the paperwork that seems to slow down the action. I realise the importance of documentation, and I cooperatively fill out the forms. But I'm always looking for efficiencies in that area that will get me out in front of the customer where I belong.

What have you enjoyed least about working freelance/your current job?

It is exciting working freelance and I have built up a substantial base of satisfied customers, however, the drawback to working freelance is the lack of security. I don't know what the future holds and sometimes that is a frightening concept. Although no job is secure nowadays, I would prefer to have a situation where I can follow a clear career path. I think even more significantly, I actually miss working with other people and having colleagues to share ideas with. I like working in a team environment.

Which particular aspect of your work do you find most frustrating?
That's an interesting question, because I am, generally speaking, a tolerant person. However, slow periods can be sources of frustration, but at times like that, I put more effort into advertising and establishing new clientele. That way, the slow periods don't last long.

Why do you want to leave your current work?
Being cabin crew is something I have always wanted to do and I am now at a point in my life where I am prepared to make the career and lifestyle change and I want to take advantage of that opportunity.

In what ways are you prepared for the career and lifestyle change?
I am prepared in many ways; I am prepared in my attitude – maturity, enthusiasm, etc. I am prepared in my life – financially able; don't have big commitments, etc. And I have the required skills and experience – customer care, teamwork, etc.

Why are you dissatisfied with your current job?
I'm not dissatisfied with my job, in many ways I am very happy where I am. I'm not looking around actively, but there are only so many extraordinary opportunities that come along in this life and this is one of them. The post you are filling calls for the skills I have and offers the scope I want.

What specific strengths did you bring to your current job that made you particularly effective?
My extensive knowledge and experience in hairdressing, coupled with my excellent customer care, and track record for accomplishment and dependability where my greatest assets, this along with the superior quality of my work and my reasonable prices enabled me to increase my customer base dramatically.

In what areas of your current work are you strongest?
I am sure it is dealing with people – my interpersonal skills are very good and I pride myself on being able to build rapport quickly with new people. I think my professional attitude and common sense approach goes down well with clients and I have always received positive feedback with regards to follow through.

Additionally, I am good at what I do. I have a natural flair for design, good judgement and am good at coming up with new ideas.

On top of those reasons, I am really enthusiastic about my work and I put a great deal of energy into it.

In what areas of your current work are you weakest?
I don't have any major weaknesses that interfere with how I do my work. The only area which can always be improved is the way to run a successful business. I have gained a great deal of business knowledge and experience during my freelancing career, such as time management, problem solving, book keeping, etc, but I feel that you can never be too good or should ever stop trying to polish your business skills.

How do you define doing a good job in your profession?
A good job in my profession is the same as doing a good job in any profession, and that is giving satisfaction and impeccable service to the client, who is always the final judge of the service. A good job also means one I'm proud of, that gives me a sense of achievement and internal satisfaction, and is in line with my professional reputation.

Why do you think you have succeeded at working freelance?
No two clients are alike, and I feel that my secret to my success is making them feel that they get individual service created for their individual needs. Second, I place strong emphasis on quality, so my work is consistently exceptional; this combined with my reasonable prices has enabled me to increase my customer base dramatically. Third, I have mastered many important business skills that bring success, such as self motivation, time management, and problem solving.

And finally, I have worked hard and committed myself. It required lots of energy but I always give 100%

What characteristics (personal qualities and skills) are necessary for success working freelance?

Working freelance, you have to be a self starter, spotting opportunities and acting on your own initiative without the support of others. You have to be self sufficient, drawing deeply on your experience and character. You need to be friendly, polite and able to talk to customers easily. You'll also need to anticipate your customer's needs and find innovative ways to get around various challenges that business life will throw at you, and be able to keep a cool head in a crisis.

What characteristics (personal qualities and skills) are necessary for success working as a hairdresser?

As it is a personal service in which the customer's satisfaction is the key to success, you need to be friendly, polite and able to talk to customers easily. You should work quickly and well with your hands, doing detailed work. A creative, artistic sense and an eye for colour and form is needed, along with an interest in fashion. Self-presentation is important so you should also be well groomed. You also need to be fit and able to stand for long periods.

How would you compare the quality of your work to your competitors/other hairdressers?

The quality of my work is to the same standard, if not better than that of my competitors. I take great pride in the quality of work I produce, and to further ensure quality I keep up to date with latest trends and fashions through subscribing to hairdressing journals.

I've always met or exceeded expectations.

How would you compare the quantity of your work to your competitors/other hairdressers?

Like the quality of the work I've produced, the overall quantity of my work has generally exceeded expectations. I set my pace according to what I can manage and what is required, and I always try to beat the clock and my own record. Due to my high energy and ability to find the fastest, most efficient way to get the work done, I'm able to keep increasing my output while maintaining quality.

How do you maintain your interest in your work?

Quite easily; when I see the clients face glow with happiness when their hair is transformed, it's very satisfying and makes the hard work worth it. Also, because no two clients are the same and each requires something different, this makes the work much more interesting as I am able to utilise my creative ability.

What have you done to make your work more effective?
To make my work more effective, I record and monitor everything I do. It ensures that I run a very professional business which is well disciplined and effective.

Details such as distance to a client's home (written in mileage), along with any factors that limited or affected the service with the client are recorded. From this data, I can identify better ways of doing things in terms of saving time and money, as a result of which I can focus more effort and energy on producing results and increasing profits.

What have you done to make your work more challenging?
I usually set myself goals to try and push myself that bit further. However, my work is challenging enough without the need to create challenges.

What have you done to make your work more interesting?
I don't need to make my work more interesting, it is interesting enough.

What is the most important thing about the work you do?
Most important is customer satisfaction, by producing the best quality work, offering the best service, and knowing that my clients are completely happy ensures that clients will return.

Is there a lot of pressure in your current work/How do you deal with this pressure?
Working freelance carries a degree of pressure that I find stimulating and enjoy working with. The pressure is usually associated with emotional clients, mind changers and lack of time. In most cases this kind of pressure provides motivation and tends to bring out the best in me.

How do you deal with mind changers and time restrictions?
When a client suddenly changes his or her mind at the last minute or when I have a big project to do and there is a tight schedule - I have to decide whether it's realistically possible to do this without the quality suffering. If I can't, I have to remain calm and try to deal with the situation in a manner that will ensure that I don't lose the client.

How do you deal with emotional clients?
When dealing with emotional clients, I have to offer comfort and assurance by listening and showing empathy whilst not getting too involved. I may feel like crying myself, but I have to bottle it all up until the end of the day.

What are some of the problems you encounter in your work/Can you think of a problem you encountered in your current job and the steps you took to overcome it/ Tell us about some obstacles you had to overcome in the past?

During the course of my freelancing experience, I have encountered various obstacles that I have had to overcome, such as supplies being delayed due to a postal strike, clients turning up late for appointments or forgetting to turn up all together.

To avoid the postal service issue re-occurring, I had to switch to a local supplier. Although the supplies were more expensive to purchase and I had to change to different brands of products, they didn't have to be delivered. I could pick the supplies up whenever demand required and the new brands, they turned out to be better than the brands I was using previously.

To ensure clients turn up, on time to their appointments, I began sending a reminder card to the client a few days before their appointment. Now, I very rarely encounter this issue.

Work Experience General

Why did you choose the hair dressing industry?

I have always been interested in hair fashion and have strong creative skill and so the decision to enter this profession came as a natural progression from that early interest.

I regard this field as a challenging and an interesting one, with many demands and a lot of hard work, but also full of opportunities to develop both my customer care and communication skills.

Out of all the positions you have held (including freelance), which position was your favourite/gave you the most satisfaction?

It's hard to pick a single favourite position because there have been aspects of every position that I've enjoyed, each for different reasons.

However, my most satisfying job to date has been my current one because it offers me the opportunity to use all of my initiative and skill to solve problems and get things done, whilst at the same time providing similar tasks to that involved in my previous positions.

Out of all the positions you have held (including freelance), which position would you say was the most boring?

I haven't found any of the work in my career boring. I've always been too busy to be bored! There has been something interesting, something that held my attention, about every position I've held, or I don't think I would have been doing the job in the first place.

Out of all the jobs/positions you have held (including freelance), which position did you least enjoy?

Each position had its different challenges, and required me to utilise my knowledge, skills and experience to meet those challenges. This made my working environment stimulating and provided opportunities to develop in many ways. So I cannot really say what position I least enjoyed as each working experience was valuable.

No matter how much the recruiters probe, don't give in.

What was the least enjoyable experience in your work experience/employment?

I cannot recall one particular moment or situation in my work history that I can say was the least enjoyable, mainly because I've always approach my career with a positive and enthusiastic attitude. When unfavourable situations occur, I see them as challenges and opportunities to learn.

> **If probed further**
> Dealing with friends and acquaintances trying to pressure me into a low price is not a great experience.

What was the most enjoyable experience in your work experience/employment?

My most enjoyable experiences are usually a result of satisfied customers. I get a sense of happiness in making people happy. That feeling of pride when you see the clients face glow with happiness when their hair has been transformed, it's very satisfying and makes me proud to see what I have done.

If asked for an example

I remember a client who came to me after wearing sewn in extensions for 3 years. The extensions had caused damage to her natural hair and spots of baldness. After carefully applying the new extensions, I sent her home with a concentrated protein spray, and after 2 weeks, her hair felt healthy again, and she had tons of new growth. Needless to say, she is VERY happy!!

Describe a time when you thought you were doing well/When were you most happy at work?

I am happy with the way things are going now; I have achieved everything I have set myself and more, and hopefully I am looking forward to an exciting new career as cabin crew.

Describe a time when you felt things were not going well?

I remember shortly after I began freelancing, there was a postal strike and my supplies were seriously delayed. I couldn't book many appointments until the stock arrived. I looked around but no local suppliers had the particular supplies that I needed. In the end I had to travel into London to pick up stock.

This experience made me realise that, although it was cheaper and more convenient to have the supplies delivered, it wasn't very reliable; which made me feel insecure, dependant on others and not in control. To avoid this issue re-occurring, I switched to a local supplier. Although the supplies were more expensive to purchase and I had to change to different brands of products, they didn't have to be delivered. I could pick the supplies up whenever demand required and the new brands, they turned out to be better than the brands I was using previously.

How many days have you had to take off due to sickness/What is your attendance record like?

I'm proud to say that my attendance record has always been very good. I'm in excellent health, I don't have any allergies and I rebound quickly. I have never had to cancel an appointment due to sickness and in the whole time I was working at Any Hair Salon, I only took 3 days off for an extremely heavy cold, but I am usually pretty resilient and, more often than not, I manage to arrange any medical appointments around my schedule.

Do you arrive at work on time?

Yes, I am usually the first to arrive in the morning and I dislike being late for anything. If I have a problem being on time – due to traffic, car trouble etc, I always call and explain the situation.

What do you feel is a satisfactory attendance record?
I believe it is every employee's responsibility to show up, on time, every work day. Days lost through sickness are unproductive and expensive and should only be taken when absolutely necessary. I think you owe it to your colleagues as well as your manager to be punctual.

Can we contact your previous employers for references/What would they say?
Yes, of course you can check my references. I'm confident that all my references will be favourable and will confirm what we've discussed here today.

What have you learned from your work experience?
There are three general things I have learned from past experience. First, if you are confused, ask – it's better to ask a dumb question than make a stupid mistake. Second, it's better to promise less and produce more than to make unrealistic forecasts. And finally, I have learned that what is good for the company is good for me.

Have you done the best work you are capable of?
That's hard to say, because I'm always striving to do better, but in doing so I increase my skills and therefore always see room for improvement. I have had some great accomplishments in my career, such as my success at working freelance, but I believe the best is yet to come.

How do you feel about your career progress to date?
In looking back over my career I am very satisfied with my progress, I have achieved all that I have set myself and more. I have identified opportunities that would stretch and develop me and have been pleased with my achievements. I have gained a great deal in terms of knowledge and experience, and I am now seeking to maintain this momentum.

do you have any regrets?
I don't regret the course of my career, because I have worked for an interesting company, with extraordinary people. I have got to learn from their advice, to better myself and ultimately, I have succeeded in my chosen profession.

If you could start your career over again, what would you do differently?
I am satisfied with the direction and progress my career has taken to date and would not do anything differently. I now look forward to progressing further.

When have you worked unsociable hours/How did you cope?

Working Freelance can involve working unsociable hours, during the busy periods. During these peak times, it is quite common for me to be working through the day, right into the late evening, typically 12 - 13 hours.

Because these are predictable periods when I expect to be kept busy, they are easy to plan for and therefore cope with.

PROFESSIONAL KNOWLEDGE AND EXPERIENCE

What is the most significant accomplishment/achievement up to this point in your career?

Although I believe my biggest accomplishments are still ahead of me, I feel my most significant accomplishment to date was rising from the receptionist and general hand to become a hairdresser. I think it demonstrates not only my growth but also the confidence my manger had in my ability. I've accomplished many things in my career since, but I still look back on that one event as the turning point and the accomplishment that made all the others possible.

In your current/past position, what problems did you come across that came as a surprise to you?

By planning ahead, I can anticipate any potential problems and be prepared to deal with them. I keep comparing my current situation against my plan and take necessary action to correct any deviation. This helps me expect and prepare for problems rather than be surprised by them.

In your current/past position, what problems did you identify that had been previously overlooked?

While I was working as a receptionist at Any Hair Salon, I identified that many clients were waiting longer than necessary when they arrived for their appointments because hairdressers had to wait for the client to arrive before they could set up the right equipment.

I realised this was because the appointment system that was being used was inefficient. When appointments were made, the only details recorded in the diary were the clients name and contact details. So from then on, I began entering as much detail as possible about the treatment required; therefore the hairdressers were able to set up the equipment before the client arrived.

This was the most sensible alternative to the way things were done previously, which resulted in a cut of waiting times. Sometimes, all that's needed is the application of common sense.

When have you experienced a pressured situation/Tell us about a time when you have been pressured by an awkward or difficult person/Tell us about a time when you had to be assertive/When have you had to say no to a client.

Example 1

I remember when an acquaintance of mine tried to pressure me into an extremely low price on the basis of friendship. I stood my ground and offered a reasonable discount and eventually she agreed to the discount I was offering, but then began insisting that I offer her the service on credit. I remained assertive and explained that I do not offer a credit facility. Eventually she accepted my reasons for not offering credit but I could sense she was not happy.

How did you cope/How did this make you feel?

This happens occasionally, so I have learnt not to take what is being said to heart and be more assertive in my response. At the end of the day, if I give in to everyone I know, I will not be in business for very long.

Example 2

I remember a client who was having a full colour and restyle done. Upon my arrival to the client's premises at 5pm, the client explained that due to last minute plans, she would need for me to finish her hair by 6pm. I explained that this would not be possible as the quality would seriously suffer. I suggested that she either re-schedule the appointment of re-organise her plans for a later time. The client disagreed with both suggestions and so I explained that I would complete her hair as quickly as I possibly could.

The client kept me continually updated with the time and then at 6pm began panicking that she was going to be really late and was going to lose her reservation. I made some further suggestions that I thought would free up some time, such as doing her make-up whilst I done her hair and also offered to give her a lift to her destination.

I completed her hair by 6.25pm and had her at the restaurant by 6.37pm, only 7 minutes late. The client was very grateful for my efforts.

How did this make you feel?

Pressured but also more focused on the task.

What did you learn?

I learnt that I really need to emphasise during the consultation how long is needed to complete the work.

Why didn't the client catch a taxi?

By the time the client rang to book a taxi, it was too late and there was a long wait for one to become available.

Tell us about a difficult situation when you pulled the team together/Describe a situation when the team fell apart. What was your role in the outcome?

I can't remember ever being in that situation, most of my colleagues at Any Hair Salon worked well together and had strong feelings of belonging to the team, however I did face something slightly similar that I could tell you about?

...I remember one situation where two of my colleagues really didn't hit it off with one another. They were constantly quarrelling and everyone had lost patience with them but no one wanted to get involved.

In the end I grasped the nettle and decided to assert myself. I was not their manager, so it was not a case of using authority. I did have to be as tactful as I could, and I began by diplomatically explaining that I acknowledged their personal dislike for each other, and then I drew upon the fact that they were both professionals and can therefore put aside their differences for the good of the salon.

I persuaded them to talk so that they could work out an effective strategy for working together. They had a pretty frank discussion and although I can't say they ended up the best of friends, they did gain more respect for one another's roles and certainly worked more productively together. I was really glad I had taken the initiative.

Tell us about a time when you have been pressured by an awkward or difficult person?

It doesn't happen very often, but I do remember when an associate of mine tried to pressure me into an extremely low price on the basis of friendship. She tried using guilt tactics but I stood my ground and offered a reasonable discount and eventually the situation was solved.

It can be a big problem when making the transition from a hobby to business, but it is up to me to let everyone know I am a professional and ask for their support.

How did you cope/How did this make you feel?

This happens occasionally, so I have learned not to take what is being said to heart and to be more assertive in my response. If I don't stand my ground, I will not be in business for very long.

What was the most difficult situation you have faced/How did you cope/How did you feel?

I remember when I was 16, my younger brother, who was about 6 years old at the time, had a convulsion. I was alone with him at the time and at first I was a little scared, but I knew I had to do something, and moved quickly to ring the emergency services.

I remained calm and as directed, I put a pillow under his head, loosened his clothes around his neck and removed nearby objects that he may damage himself on. His tongue was floppy so was blocking the hole in his throat, which caused him to stop breathing. I was told not to put my finger in his mouth as he may bite it off; instead I was to roll him onto his side and wait for him to regain consciousness. I took several deep breaths and after a couple of minutes, he regained consciousness and the ambulance arrived.

This was the most worrying experience I have had to deal with, but I remained calm and managed to keep my emotions under control.

What has been the biggest disappointment of your career?

I couldn't say that I have had any big disappointments in my career. I've been doing the type of work I like and that makes good use of my knowledge and experience. However I was a little let down when I didn't get onto a part time hairdressing course after leaving school and yet I ended up enjoying myself and doing well anyway, and eventually I managed to get myself on the course.

Naturally, if I don't get this job, it will be my biggest disappointment; it is something I really want.

What did you learn from the experience?

My disappointment over this course made me start applying early to the courses that interested me so that I could avoid a further disappointment. I have never come across this problem since.

Describe a time when you've had to deal with an angry or upset customer/How did you resolve the situation?
I had a client who was booked in for highlights, but after examining her hair, I noticed she had a dry blistery scalp. As the health of my clients is important to me, I was not prepared to carry out the treatment as it may worsen the problem. The client was understandably very upset.

I listened to what she had to say and then apologised for the inconvenience. When I had managed to calm her down, I was able to explain that I was not prepared to take the risk for her own protection and explained that I would be happy to return to carry out the procedure once her scalp had healed. Although the client felt very disappointed, she waited several days. During this time, her scalp had healed and I was able to return to carry out the service.

What was wrong with her scalp?
The client had had an adverse reaction to a product that she had used a few days prior.

How did you approach the conversation?
I was polite, sympathetic and professional.

How did it make you feel?
Health and safety is an important issue and one I take seriously. So although I felt disappointed for the client, I did not feel bad because I done what I felt was right.

Tell us about a time when you were confronted by someone shouting at or being abusive toward you/How did you cope/How did this make you feel?
I have not been put in such a situation before mainly because I do not give people reasons to be that away inclined but, in being faced with this situation I would always take the person concerned into a private area where I can calm things down and talk to them in private.

How exactly would you deal with them?
If available, I would offer a cup or tea, and then I would listen to what they have to say.

I would let them get the whole thing off their chest and show that I am listening by; asking for clarification where appropriate, summarising, using the appropriate body language, and making notes where appropriate.

I would then investigate the facts because, whatever I feel personally about the situation, I cannot deny their feelings of anger or disappointment and whether the person is justified or not, something has angered them, so whatever it was could anger someone else. I need to find out what has happened and, learn from it.

If at any point I feel uncomfortable or even in danger when someone is shouting or showing signs of becoming physically aggressive, I would simply walk away. I would explain my action and specify the consequences of certain behaviour. If I judge it to be necessary, I would not hesitate to ask for help.

What has been your greatest professional mistake/What was the biggest mistake you have ever made?
The biggest mistake was providing my service to a friend on credit. Not only was it extremely difficult to retrieve the money, but once the message got around, everybody else began expecting the same treatment.

Unfortunately, it really was my fault. I learned from the experience and I have never made the same mistake since.

How have you benefited/learned from your mistakes?
I have learned a lot from mistakes, either my own or those of others. Whenever I make a mistake, I acknowledge the error, and use it as a lesson to keep me from making the same mistake again. That way I never repeat mistakes and always anticipate potential problems. We all make mistakes; it's what we do with the lessons learned from our mistakes that determine our success in life.

For example... The mistake I made in providing my service to a friend on credit made me think twice before giving anyone credit in the future, I have never made the same mistake since.

How have you benefited/learned from your disappointments?
I have learned a lot from disappointments, either my own or those of others. I wouldn't call them disappointments as such, just temporary setbacks. Whenever I encounter disappointment, my first task is to look at what happened, why it happened, and how I would do things differently in each stage should the same set of circumstances appear again. That way I never repeat mistakes and always anticipate potential problems.

Or

I treat every disappointment as a learning experience. Whenever I have a disappointment, my first task is to analyse what went wrong and how it could have been prevented. That way, I put disappointment behind me and am ready with renewed confidence and understanding to face the new day's problems.

How do you prepare yourself for potential problems?
I prepare for potential problems by analysing past problems. In any case, I think of problems as opportunities to be creative.

What do you do when you have trouble solving a problem?
One thing I don't do is ignore it and hope it will go away. I stand back and examine the problem. I make a list of possible solutions, weighing both the consequences and cost of each solution to determine the best course of action. I then present my planned solution to those who will be affected by it and seek advice and/or approval.

How do you handle failure?
Naturally failing hurts my feelings however, I am not one to give up quickly. I treat every failing as a learning experience; I look at what went wrong, why it went wrong, and how I would do things differently should the same set of circumstances appear again. That way, I put failure behind me and am ready with renewed confidence and understanding.

What have been the biggest frustrations in your career?
I've always approached my career with enthusiasm, so I really haven't experienced much frustration. When I do find myself up against a source of frustration, I convert it into an opportunity to prove myself and set an example for others to follow.

How do you approach difficult situations?

I approach difficult situations in a calm and objective way and am polite yet resolute when handling a difficult customer. I try to seek acceptable outcomes and am undaunted if solutions cannot always be found.

How often have you missed deadlines and what were the outcomes?

I rarely miss deadlines, owing to my planning and organising skills and general project management abilities. My experience plays an important role in anticipating the problems and prevention of the things that could go wrong. Good planning and effective control over the work is the most effective weapon in the battle with time and mounting costs.

Give me an example of a problem you encountered that didn't work out

My bank returned my client's cheque to me through lack of funds. I was sure this was a mistake caused through an oversight on the part of my client. I tried ringing the client on several occasions so that I could explain the situation and agree a time when I would collect the money. Failing that, I went round to the client's house. I left a note but never heard back. At this point, I had to decide whether to write off the debt and blacklist the client or visit the Citizens' Advice Bureau for advice on retrieving the funds. After careful consideration of all the factors involved, I decided to write the debt off. I learned from the experience and I now wait for the funds to clear before carrying out a service.

Tell us about a time when you solved a customer problem

I solve customer problems all the time, however, I remember one problem in particular. I had a client who had previously worn sewn in extensions for 3 years, which had caused damage to the natural hair and spots of baldness. After carefully applying the new extensions, I sent her home with a concentrated protein spray, and after 2 weeks, her hair felt healthy again, and she had tons of new growth. Needless to say, she is VERY happy!!

Please briefly relate an experience where you were especially pleased with the service/assistance you were able to give someone/When have you gone out of your way for a client?

Example 1

I remember a client was asking for a particular product that she had been recommended. The client had searched around for this product but hadn't had any luck in tracking it down. I knew I could get this product from the wholesalers where I collected my supplies from but it was not available for purchase by the general public, so I offered to help her by collecting the product for her. She was very happy and grateful for my efforts, which gave me a sense of self satisfaction.

Example 2

When I first went freelance, the process of my work was to provide the service within the client's home or chosen premises. I encountered a problem when one of my clients was unable to have the service carried out in her home because it was in the process of being redecorated. I rang a contact I had within a local salon and was able to arrange to carry out the service within the salon for a small fee. This worked out really well because the salon was in a location that was convenient for both myself and the client to travel to.

How do you deal with a difficult customer?

Example 1

I remember when I had a consultation with a client and we agreed on the colour and style she wanted to have done. When her appointment date came round, she had decided to go for something completely different. As a result, I had to reschedule her appointment in order to purchase different products. At times like this, I have to be patient, calm, professional and understanding.

How do you prevent this situation re-occurring?

I have to really emphasise during the consultation how important it is that the client keeps me informed of any changes.

Example 2

I recall a time when I had carried out a cut and highlights on a client, it had taken me about 2 and a half hours to complete and I was satisfied with the final result and thought it was one of the best I had done. This however was not consistent with the clients feelings as she didn't feel it suited her and wasn't happy with the final result. After some deliberation, she insisted on having her hair put back t its original colour. She apologised for having wasted my efforts but agreed to pay me for my time. She later rescheduled an appointment for a different colour and was satisfied with the final result.

How did this make you feel?
At first I was disappointed, but this made me realise that what I like is not necessarily what someone else will like. My main concern is that I leave the client happy and content.

Did you try to persuade her to keep the highlights?
Yes, I explained that it was probably just the initial shock and therefore she should give herself a few days to see if she gets used to the colour and if she still didn't like it after this time, I would happily return to remove the colour.

How do you prevent this situation re-occurring?
I have to really emphasise during the consultation that the results of a different colour, whether it be partial highlights or full head of colour, will create a dramatic result and so are they absolutely sure they want to go ahead. I also began using wigs and hairpieces to give an example of what the final result will look like, that way, I am sure they are completely happy to go ahead.

When have you handled a customer complaint?

I remember when I was working on reception at Any Hair Salon and a client rang to complain about a perm that she had had done. I knew the customer wasn't happy, so I gave her chance to talk while I listened. This seemed to calm her down. Once she had finished what she wanted to say, I told her that I could understand her disappointment and apologised for the situation.

I immediately offered her an appointment so that the stylist could examine her hair and identify the cause of the problem and if necessary re-perm the dropped side. The client said that would be fine. I thanked her for her understanding and immediately booked her an appointment.

The client later told me that I was very caring and professional and she later sent a complimentary letter about me to the salon manager.

It made me feel good that I was able to turn her experience into a positive one and as a direct result, the client became a regular visitor to the salon.

Why had the perm dropped?

The client's hair was fairly fine and one side had simply taken better than the other.

Tell us about the biggest challenge you have faced/How did you respond to that challenge?

To be honest – giving up smoking was the biggest challenge. I never thought I could do it and I had had dozens of attempts that ended in failure. It isn't just the fact that I don't smoke any more. I have gained so much personal insight and I deal with potentially stressful situations at work so much more effectively now, I feel more energetic, more mentally alert and far calmer now than I ever did before.

Have you ever misinterpreted any instructions, message or information/What was the outcome of those situations?

No, I am pleased to say that I haven't. I always devote my exclusive attention to the person speaking to me. That way most misunderstandings can be eliminated and effective communication established. I notice that most poor listeners, when they are not talking, are busy rehearsing what they are going to say next. That way it is very difficult to exchange ideas and messages.

PERSONAL TRAITS AND SKILLS
My Views

What are your best qualities/greatest strengths?

I have very good interpersonal skills and I pride myself on being able to build rapport quickly with new people. To me, establishing rapport seems to be a natural tendency. In fact, at Any Hair Salon, I was often asked to carry out the shampoo because the manager knew I would make the clients feel welcome and important.

I am always professional and adopt a mature approach to my work. I keep calm and don't let attention to detail slip when there is a lot of pressure and can be relied on to pull with the team when it's facing any kind of challenge.

I'm driven to achieve, to surpass my most recent record, so you'll never see me deliver merely acceptable performance and communicate well with my superiors and colleagues at all times,

I feel that for the above reasons I would be successful as cabin crew and would be a valuable asset to XYZ Airlines.

What qualities are you not so proud of/ What is your greatest weakness?

I can, on occasion, be a bit of a perfectionist. I tend to spend longer than necessary making sure that things are perfect and sometimes get a little frustrated if I don't achieve excellence. I did learn early on in my career that this slows output, but on the other hand, without such attention to detail, the consistency and accuracy of my work could be affected. It is a difficult balancing act but I am working on finding a more balanced approach, for example being contempt with satisfactory standards.

In what way are you a perfectionist?

I set myself high standards, which means I am not satisfied until I have surpassed satisfactory standards.

What are your 3 greatest strengths and weaknesses?
Strengths
Delivering customer care
Communication skills
Managing adversity

Weaknesses
I expect high standards
I sometimes work too hard
It's hard to think of anything which comes to mind, however if I had to choose a third weakness, it would be chocolate.

How have you changed in the last 5 years?
I feel like I have matured-rather than aged 5 years. The skills I have acquired and the qualities I have developed have changed me enormously and I know there are parts of me that are not being utilised half as effectively as they could be.

Each position I have carried out has given me an opportunity to develop my communication, interpersonal and problem solving skills, I have learnt how to work successfully with others, how to deal effectively with suppliers and clients and how to motivate and be motivated. I have also greatly enhanced my people management and leadership skills. All of these will benefit my performance as a cabin crew member.

Do you consider yourself a future, present, or past orientated person?
I try to live in the present, thinking in terms of what needs to be done now, instead of thinking about the past or worrying about the future. The past experiences are always valuable, and making plans for the future is an important business activity, but I endeavour to concentrate my efforts on current problems and issues.

Would you classify yourself as a hard-working or relatively laid back?
When it comes to my job, I don't have time to be laid back. When I'm at work, I always give my best and try to achieve as much as possible. Of course, it is necessary to slow down from time to time to analyse my performance and plan future activities. Then, the hard driving starts again. I have always been self-motivated and not to work hard would be against my personal beliefs.

Are you an introvert or extrovert?

I am quite extrovert, but I'm not so dependant upon other people that I get withdrawal symptoms when left alone.

or

I enjoy company, but can easily spend time alone and enjoy that too. I am by no means cautious but I feel no compulsion to take risks or to involve myself in situations where the spotlight is on me.

Do you have an analytical mind?

In the sense that I can identify problems and work out solutions to them, yes. I have above average analytical skills. Like everything else, good analytical skills come through practice, through using that amazing computer between your ears on a regular basis. That's why I'm looking for work that requires me to think and act.

Rate yourself on a scale from 1 to 10

I would rate myself as an 8. I always give my best, but in doing so I increase my skills and therefore always see room for improvement.

Do you consider yourself assertive or aggressive?

I think the word I would use to describe myself would be assertive, rather than aggressive. When I think of an aggressive person, I think of someone who bullies or steamrolls others to get his or her way. Being assertive, on the other hand, allows me to make my ideas known without disparaging the ideas and opinions of others. It allows for a mutually fulfilling, two way exchange, without anyone being put down or attacked.

Or

I would consider myself to be assertive rather than aggressive. I am not afraid to be honest and direct, even if I think that the response is not going to be popular. However, directness doesn't mean rudeness or an absence of tact. I accept my own good and bad characteristics and do not feel the need to put others down, or to win. I acknowledge my own needs and opinions directly and openly, risking rejection or refusal. My self esteem doesn't depend on the approval of others, but I can respond sincerely to them.

Tell us about a time when you have had to be assertive?
I have to be assertive with friends and associates of mine who try to pressure me into low prices. Being assertive in this situation is especially challenging because I know the individual concerned.

Do you consider yourself a smart person?
Yes. That means I'm smart enough to know my opinion is biased. The kind of intelligence required on the job isn't always measured by IQ. Only through coping with different situations and interacting with other people can intelligence truly be judged. By these criteria, I'm above average in intelligence.

When it comes to working with people, solving business problems, and making decisions – especially those related to the job – I'm as good as or better than anyone else. There are many things I don't know, but I can learn. In that way, a smart person is one who asks questions, listens carefully, and realises nobody knows everything.

Or

To me, smart people are not necessarily the ones with high IQs. Education and intelligence is the ability to meet life's situations and perform in the job to the best of one's abilities. We show our value by the way we deal with people, approach business problems and make decisions.

With that in mind and without any false modesty I would consider myself a smart person. Of course, there are many things I don't know, but I make constant learning and self-improvement my main goal. To me, to be smart means to ask questions, listen to what people say, apply knowledge and know-how to problems and learn from my own and, preferably, from other people's mistakes.

What do you do when you find it difficult to do your best work?
I rarely find it difficult to do my best work, I am always motivated to give my best efforts, and there are always opportunities to contribute when you stay alert. When for various reasons, it becomes difficult to do my best work, I find myself driving to produce, to maintain my record of success.

When do you tend to do your best work, in the morning or in the afternoon?
The time of day usually has no impact on my efficiency and energy level, but I prefer morning hours for major tasks, and late afternoon or early evening for planning, design and catching up on paperwork. I rarely get tired, even when I work overtime – it's just that some periods during the day are better suited for particular activities.

What motivates you to work hard?
I have always been self motivated. I like that winning feeling when I do a good job and the sense of achievement and job satisfaction motivate me to make even bigger efforts. I also like being surrounded by bright people who are capable, hard working and good team players; the energy and creativity people can activate in each other is amazing.

Other great motivators include: Daily challenges, personal growth, accepting responsibility, looking forward to achieving goals, encouragement to use creativity and initiative in finding new ways to do things and finally, respect for a job well done.

Name 5 things that motivate you
Tangible results
The opportunity to work as part of a talented team of individuals
Daily challenges
Personal growth
Encouragement to use creativity and initiative in finding new ways to do things

So money doesn't motivate you?
Although I consider remuneration an important motivational factor, it is a secondary importance. The job itself, its tasks, the work environment and the opportunity to learn and participate in new and exciting developments, and become an efficient member of the team, are to me the most significant aspects of a job.

Are you a self starter?

Yes I am. I rarely need others to motivate me, as I am very directed by my own career and am the sort of person who enjoys taking the initiative. I can set expectations for my work that are usually higher than others set for me, and I can achieve them. I'm a quick study and can be up and running with a minimum of instruction and training.

Or

Yes, I do consider myself a self starter. I never rely on someone else's initiative, I take the initiative myself. As a self starter, I can identify problems, devise a plan of action and assume full responsibility for my activities and the successful completion of required tasks.

How do you feel about routine tasks and irregular hours?

I accept that every role carries with it a certain amount of routine in order to get the job done. If my job involves repetitive work, it is my responsibility to carry it out to the best of my abilities. As for irregular hours I would expect to have an indication of my core hours but will work the hours that are necessary in order to fulfill the requirements of the role.

Change drives this organisation, how flexible are you/How do you deal with change?

I positively thrive on change. I like to know that each day is going to be very different, with its own set of decisions to make and problems to solve.

When have you had to face major changes in your personal life or work?

The biggest change I have faced was going freelance. Being responsible for organising my own time, finding my own clients and dealing with my own accounts is very different from working in a salon. Being freelance also means no colleagues, which was the biggest and hardest change. However, I found the change very refreshing and a great challenge; as well as learning to be independent, I have learned, responsibility, discipline, and hard work. Each of which will benefit my performance as a cabin crew member.

Do you get bored doing the same work over and over again/Do you get bored with detail?
No. Work is not necessarily entertaining; it is something that must be routinely and successfully accomplished time after time. That's why it is called work and why I am being paid to do it. Sometimes you just have to set your preferences aside and focus on what needs to be done – even if it isn't something new and exciting.

How often do you loose your temper?
I am patient, understanding, and easy to deal with and never lose my temper. I regard that sort of behaviour as counterproductive and inappropriate. By losing your temper, you cannot possibly resolve a problem – you can only make it worse. Even if you're completely right, losing your temper often destroys your ability to convince others that you are right. Maintaining an open and positive approach to problems and potential conflicts, helps to control temper.

What makes you angry/Tell us about the last time you felt angry/What makes you impatient/Tell us about the last time you felt impatient.
Not much makes me angry or impatient, however I understand that situations can occur occasionally, but instead of getting angry or impatient, I exert my energy into maintaining my professional approach and conduct.

Or

That's an interesting question, because I am, generally speaking, a tolerant person and I bear troubles calmly. Instead of getting angry or impatient, I use the opportunity to look at my own attitude and take responsibility for my own thoughts, so I begin to focus on the positives, on how I am really feeling beneath all that anger. The results are quite dramatic, my whole demeanour changes very rapidly, I become aware that I am in control. Now I know that in any given set of circumstances, I have the freedom to choose my attitude and control my own thoughts.

What are some of the things that bother you?
I enjoy my work and believe in giving value to my employer. Dealing with clock watchers and the ones who regularly get sick on Mondays and Friday's concerns me, but it's not something that gets me angry or anything like that.

How do you deal with these types of people?

I talk to them to find out if there is any resolve to problems which they may be encountering.

Can you take instructions and not feel upset or hurt?

Yes, I take instructions well and I recognise that it comes in two varieties, depending on the circumstances. There is carefully explained instructions then there are those times when, as a result of deadlines and other pressures the instruction might be brief and to the point. While I have seen some people get upset with that, personally I've always understood that there are probably other considerations I am not aware of. So I listen very carefully to directions and always keep my superior informed of my actions.

How do you react to constructive criticism?

Criticism is vital to my continued growth, and I welcome constructive criticism that helps me operate better or produce better results. However, it is important for me to understand where my critic is coming from so that I know how to apply the feedback.

Describe a situation when your work or idea was criticised

Example 1

I remember when I was working at Any Hair Salon and I suggested to my manager that the salon would benefit from offering a nail service as an addition to the current services that were currently offered as it would increase clientele and revenue.

My manager was not enthusiastic and dismissed the idea as she said it would incur a lot of extra overheads for the salon and also, she didn't want the extra responsibility of adding a new service.

After this discussion, I went away and done some research into the costs involved, I visited salons and suppliers for price lists and spoke to clients about what they thought of the idea and would they be inclined to use the service. I received some very positive feedback from this research and so decided to re-approach my manager with the information.

She spent some time looking over the information and done some research herself and also came back with positive results and subsequently agreed with the idea. A couple of months later, the service was added and a nail technician was hired. The result was, as expected, a dramatic increase in new clientele and revenue.

Why didn't your manager think of this idea?
She thought there would be a lot of extra costs and responsibilities involved, she later realised that the costs were not very high and neither were the responsibilities.

How did she initially respond to your idea?
She explained that she was happy to see that I was enthusiastic about making the salon better but it was not something she was going to consider at that time.

How did you respond to the criticism?
I thanked her for her time and explained that as I thought it was a good idea worth considering, I thought I would mention it.

How did it make you feel?
I did not take it to heart as I felt it was constructive criticism and I realise now that I should have gathered facts and figures before I approached her with my idea.

Why didn't you do research before approaching her with your idea?
I realise now that that is what I should have done, this is what I learnt from the experience.

Why did you suggest a nail service in particular?
I had noticed that a lot of our clients had nail extensions, this meant that we already had potential clients coming into the salon before even advertising the service.

Example 2
I remember when I was holding a consultation with a client and the client asked for my opinion on what hair colour I thought would suit her. I examined her eyes and skin tone and then suggested that I thought a warm mahogany colour would suit her as it would really emphasise the colour of her eyes and compliment her warm complexion. The colour was completely different to what she currently had and she didn't approve to say the least. I gave her a strand of extension hair in the colour I had recommended and suggested that she take it away with her and maybe she would grow to like it. A couple of weeks later, she booked into the salon for a colour change and was pleasantly surprised with the final result and subsequently apologised for her initial reaction and harsh criticism.

Why did she change her mind?

When she left the salon, she told her friends about my suggestion and they agreed, this made her reconsider and later agreed herself. Also, the strand of extension hair I gave her had a positive impact.

How did she respond initially to your suggestion?

She gasped and said no way, she said it was a horrible colour and far too dark.

How did it make you feel?

I did not take it to heart because I knew that my suggestion would be a bit of a shock and also, I knew that what I like is not necessarily what someone else will like.

How do you deal with criticism/How do you react to criticism that is unwarranted?

I try to see criticism as useful feedback on what I've done. When someone lets me have it, either fairly or unfairly, constructively or unconstructively, I first consider who is making the charges. It is important for me that I know where the critic is coming from, so that I know how to apply the feedback.

I look for the good in what the other person is saying. I don't read between the lines, nor add meaning or implications where none were intended. When the other person has finished, I ask any questions that are needed and seek recommendations or ideas that will readily improve the situation.

I would express regret over the situation then thank the person for raising the issue. If I intend to act on what I've heard, I let the other person know.

How would you react if you were criticised about your contribution?

Of course no one is perfect and there is always room for improvement. I welcome the opportunity to improve my performance.

How do you handle personal criticism?

As long as the criticism is fair and constructive, I try to listen to it and remain gracious. I thank them for their candid feedback, and modify my future behaviour accordingly.

And what do you do if the criticism is not fair or constructive?
I don't pay much attention to unwarranted criticism. I remain gracious and thank them for their input and concern.

How do you manage stress?
I always take time at the end of the day to reflect upon the days events and to analyse what I could have done better. When I notice prolonged problems, I take action to bring about change. I have found that taking time to reflect is a key element to managing stress.

Furthermore, I practise stress management through relaxation, rest and regular exercise and I avoid substances that can negatively affect my good health, such as cigarettes, alcohol and fast food.

I regularly go swimming and perform yoga and relaxation techniques which really help me to unwind and get ready for another day at work.

What are the 3 most important skills that you have developed in your career so far?
Number one is easy; I've significantly improved my communication and interpersonal skills - working with colleagues, dealing with suppliers and members of the public. Number two; I've developed my problem solving skills – anticipating as well as solving problems, and as for number three; I've greatly enhanced my people management and leadership skills.

Each of these will transfer well and benefit my performance as a cabin crew member.

What don't you like to do?
I don't particularly enjoy doing paperwork, which seems to slow down the action. However, I realise the importance of documentation, so I cooperatively fill out any forms. But I'm always looking for efficiencies in that area that will get me out in front of the customer where I belong.

When there's something disagreeable to be done, I try to get it out of the way first.

What are some of the things you find difficult to do?
I find it difficult to do nothing; I have to be doing something.

What are your likes?

I like challenges. I always set personal goals to try and push myself that bit further and to feel I've achieved something.

What sorts of challenges do you like?

I enjoy challenges that require me to use my initiative and problem solving skills.

What are your dislikes?

I try to be honest and act with integrity. I dislike it when others lie, blame or don't show the same commitment to the task or the company as I do.

How do you deal with these people?

I deal with these people in a professional and assertive manner and address the issues that are creating problems and conflict. Hopefully, by bringing the issues to the surface, this can help resolve the matter.

What do you consider yourself good at doing?

I consider myself good at providing exceptional customer care and working well under pressure.

How would you describe yourself/What sort of person are you?

I am a friendly, approachable person who has a genuine interest in people. I readily adapt to new people and work environments, and demonstrate an understanding of how to blend my personality with those possessed by other people. I am always professional and adopt a mature approach to my work. I am a rational, sensible and calm individual and can maintain my standards when under pressure. I work well on my own initiative as well as a team player and I deliver consistently excellent customer service.

If you had to characterise yourself in one sentence, what would you say?

I am a professional, friendly, confident, diplomatic person who has good communication, customer care and teamwork skills. However, I don't feel to characterise myself in one sentence is enough.

Describe yourself in 3 words.

Composed, personable and energetic.

However, I don't feel to characterise myself in 3 word(s) is enough.

What is your most memorable characteristic/What makes you stand out from the crowd?

My most memorable attribute is my ability to remain calm and level headed while under pressure. I am a very rational person and never let my emotions cloud my rational thought processes.

I can remain calm when people around me are getting agitated and I am often the person who gets called on when there is a problem. On many occasions throughout my career and personal life I have demonstrated this capability. For instance...

I remember when I was 16, my younger brother, who was about 6 years old at the time, had a convulsion. I remained calm and moved quickly to ring the emergency services. This was the most worrying experience I have had to deal with, but I remained calm and managed to keep my emotions under control.

How do you remain rational?

By remaining positive, using my common sense and initiative and keeping my emotions under control.

Do you work well under pressure/Can you work under pressure?

I positively thrive on pressure – it makes me alert and very motivated and can force the release of untapped reserves of energy and initiative. However, there are limits and I try to avoid pressure becoming too great by enhancing my skills for dealing with pressure, re-evaluating my reaction to those situations, events, people or tasks which appear threatening to me, and increasing my fitness to cope; as a result, I avoid pressure becoming problematic.

How do you re-evaluate your reaction to threatening situations?

Imagining negative images creates a negative attitude, so it is important to react positively by replacing these negative images with positive ones. How you react to pressure depends very much on how you perceive it.

How does fitness enable you to cope?

A strong body means a strong mind and thus stamina is important both physically and mentally.

How well do you lead people?

I've experienced good results from the leadership side of my work. I can communicate company goals and motivate people to produce. I'm pleased that those I initially trained and supervised eventually moved on to positions of greater responsibilities.

What would you say is your leadership style?

I adopt a varied style of leadership dependent upon the situation. However, generally speaking, I believe I am the kind of leader that draws colleagues with me, rather than one who pushes them from behind. I suppose I would describe myself as a bit of a shaper, good with new ideas and quick to spot how to delegate effectively and take on appropriate work myself.

Other People's Views

How would a friend describe you?

They would say I am easy to get on with, have a good sense of humour, am quite outgoing, and am generally cheerful. They would also say I am someone who keeps personal commitments, protects personal confidences, and makes the time to help people.

How would an enemy describe your character?

I don't have enemies that I know of, but if I did have, I suppose they might say that I am tenacious, brave, and driven.

Why Tenacious

I am certainly not a person to give in without a struggle, but on the other hand, I'm quite realistic about my limits.

Why Brave

I am prepared to confront issues when there is a need, and I'm not too concerned, but I weigh the consequences and don't act irresponsibly.

Why Driven

I know how to push for what I want, but can back off when it is advisable to do so.

Do you have a competitive nature?
Yes, a competitive nature is necessary to be successful in a corporate environment, but competitiveness doesn't mean steamrolling others to get my way. I am always competing with myself, trying to break my own record – to do something better and faster than the last time.

What would colleagues say about you/What do other people think of the way you work/What do others think are your best qualities/strengths?
It's a bit difficult to predict their response to this question. Judging by the successful and professional relationship I had with my colleagues, I would expect to be portrayed as hard working, motivated, a good communicator and a person of high integrity and moral. I believe they would also tell you that I am easy to get on with and am usually cheerful.

The formal feedback from my superiors was always very positive and they will tell you that I am a committed and enthusiastic member of the team, and am good with customers, I work well on my own initiative as well as with the team, I keep calm and don't let attention to detail slip when there is a lot of pressure and can be relied on to pull with the team when facing any kind of challenge.

Are you sure they would be that positive – there must be aspects of your personality that some of them would be less enthusiastic about?
I am sure that my colleagues would agree with what I have said as we had a successful and professional working relationship.

How well did superiors rate your job performance/ What did superiors think are your strengths/ In what areas have you received compliments from superiors?
My superiors always rated my job performance well, formally and informally. In fact, I was always rated as being capable of accepting further responsibilities. I received particularly favourable evaluations in the areas of customer care and working well with co workers. I have also received high ratings in the area of initiative and enthusiasm, because I look at each situation as a potentially exciting challenge, my superior's say I create excitement in other team members, which results in a greater team effort and higher output.

What did superiors think are your weaknesses?

What might be perceived by some as weaknesses are really my strengths, for example, I occasionally received comments about working too hard and putting in too many hours. They said that they thought I might be over-exerting myself and may burn myself out.

I see it as dedication and enthusiasm for my career and I personally don't feel I over-exert myself. Outside of work, I take time to relax and regularly go swimming, and practice yoga routines. This gives me a break from the work environment and keeps me stimulated.

COMMUNICATION/INTERPERSONAL SKILLS

When have you shown good communication/interpersonal skills?

In my work, I have to deal with people on a daily basis, so being able to communicate well, is a necessary part of my job.

My style of communication should establish a professional and caring relationship with the client. While the exact style that I use differs according to each individual, I must be courteous, friendly and professional, no matter who the client is or what my personal feelings are and I must not air my stresses or personal grievances with or in front of the client.

I recognise that these are key skills for a professional and successful business relationship.

How important is communication when dealing with your clients?

Unless you are aware of your client's wishes you will not be able to work towards satisfying them. Communication is the key.

or

Effective communication between me and the client is essential. Failure to communicate effectively with the client may result in failure to fulfil the client's wishes and loss of business.

What action do you take if there are members of your team who really don't get on with one another, to the point where this is affecting other staff and performance?

Most of my colleagues at Any Hair Salon worked well together and had strong feelings of belonging to the team. However, I do remember one situation where two of my colleagues really didn't hit it off with one another. They were constantly quarrelling and everyone had lost patience with them but no one wanted to get involved.

In the end I grasped the nettle and decided to assert myself. I was not their manager, so it was not a case of using authority. I did have to be as tactful as I could, and I began by diplomatically explaining that I acknowledged their personal dislike for each other, and then I drew upon the fact that they were both professionals and can therefore put aside their differences for the good of the salon. I persuaded them to talk so that they could work out an effective strategy for working together. They had a pretty frank discussion and although I can't say they ended up the best of friends, they did gain more respect for one another's roles and certainly worked more productively together. I was really glad I had taken the initiative.

What would you do if no amount of effort on your part solved the problem?
If after talking to them nothing changes or the situation worsens, I would need to consider seeking advice from a senior member of staff.

What was the toughest communication problem you have faced?
When I was visiting Gambia, I became acquainted with a French speaking lady. She understood my French, the little amount I knew, but she didn't really understand English. Unfortunately, the amount of French I knew wasn't enough to get me through a whole conversation, so I had to improvise.

To ensure she could understand, I used French wherever possible, was careful to avoid slang, jargon, acronyms, buzzwords, clichés, and colloquialisms and made more use of facial expressions and hand gestures. At first, it was a little tricky trying to find imaginative ways to communicate, but as time went on, it became much easier. Now when I encounter this type of communication barrier, I am much more confident in my ability to cope.

Tell us about a time that you had to be tactful
I have to be tactful all the time in my work. Clients tell hairdressers all sorts of very personal things, particularly when they are in their own home and they know the information is confidential. This means I have to be discreet with personal issues, sensitive to problems and diplomatic in my response, whilst not getting too involved.

How confident are you about addressing a group?
I used to be nervous about speaking in front of a group, yet I found that preparation, practice and knowing my subject helped me overcome this, I now have no problem addressing a group.

How do you handle conflict/If you have a disagreement with a colleague, how do you handle it?
Collaborating is a problem solving approach, based on the principle that conflict can be managed so that nobody loses completely. I try to use this approach when dealing with conflict, because it does not focus on right or wrong, or who is to blame, but sees defining the problem and seeking a solution as a joint activity. Sometimes solutions emerge that neither side would have come up with independently. It is both analytical and flexible. You listen to others points of view and work to find a solution that is as good as it can be.

Collaborating in problem solving is the most productive way to handle conflict. The approach works towards a win-win situation, in which all those involved feel as if they have gained something in the process.

To handle a conflict situation
- Acknowledge the conflict exists
- Tackle conflict early to avoid it escalating
- Plan how to deal with the conflict
- Think it through
- Don't handle conflict in public/Set the scene/Identify common ground
- Raise the issue/Open it up/Talk it through/Get more information/Agree on what the problem is
- Refrain from offering my own opinion before understanding the full picture
- Try to avoid instinctive reactions
- Stay assertive
- Don't take it personally (unless it is personal)
- Don't fight anger with anger
- Pay attention to verbal and non-verbal communication
- Generate ideas

- Find solutions
- Agree on further action

Not all conflict at work is necessarily bad. People sometimes believe that conflict means there is a breakdown in communications or that one party simply doesn't get it. Even fully functional, rational people can view situations differently. Thus conflict may help bring different views and opinions to the surface so that ultimately a team can achieve great synergy and the desired results.

DECISION MAKING

Do you consider yourself to be thoughtful and analytical or do you usually make up your mind fast?
I would consider myself a little bit of both, I put thought and planning into any decision I make while having an awareness of the timescales involved.

What decisions do you dislike making?
The kinds of decisions I dislike making, are the ones which result in customer dissatisfaction, such as having to cancel or postpone an appointment for example. When the client is dissatisfied, I feel dissatisfied. However, I accept that these kinds of decisions cannot always be avoided, and so I deal with them efficiently as they arise and try to arrive at a solution that produces the best results for the company while minimising the effects on the customer.

What decisions do you find most difficult?
It's not that I have difficulties making decisions – some just require more consideration than others.

What was the most difficult decision you have made?
The decision to leave the comfort and security of my full time job to become freelance was definitely the hardest I have had to make. Making the right decision required a lot of fore thought and looking at best – and worst case scenarios extensively before making my decision.

I carried out independent research and already had a few clients to start off with, but still found the decision difficult because I knew that, at the end of the day, there are no guarantees that people will use the service.

Thankfully I went ahead and the outcome was positive.

How do you go about making important decisions?
Before I act, I think. I evaluate my options and examine them objectively, weighing up possible outcomes, pros and cons, etc. I then rely on past experiences, company policies, intuition and common sense to guide me to a decision. I present my planned solution to those who will be affected by it - the staff, as well as those who will be called upon to explain my decision - my superiors. I then implement appropriate input and suggestions, where necessary. I believe in immediate but realistic solutions to problems.

Or

Before making an important decision, I take three basic steps. First, I analyse all aspects of the issue and all possible consequences. Second, I try to anticipate potential problems that can affect the decision or be caused by it. Third, I talk to people who would be affected by that decision and get their input. By following these rules I make sure that the right decision is made.

Obviously, no one can tell you why you want the job, but it is crucial you consider this question both from your own, and the airline's perspective. If for example all you want is travel, and you cannot convince your recruiters that you would enjoy looking after their passengers, being a member of their cabin crew team, and being with their organisation, then you are probably ruling yourself out of contention!

When asked about your own personal qualities, it is sensible to emphasise those that are relevant to the role. Candidates who have not considered how the job will impact on their life will seem naive.

If you are asked about disadvantages, it would be best to choose the main drawbacks for your own circumstances, and then be prepared to say how you intend to overcome them!

Asking you to compare yourself with other candidates is unfair, but if this does come up you should stress your best qualities and why these would enable you to make a positive contribution to the airline's fortunes, rather than being negative about others.

KNOWLEDGE AND SUITABILITY FOR THE JOB
Cabin Crew

What kind of individual do you think we are looking for to fill this role?
I believe you are looking for an individual who has good communication, teamwork, and customer care skills and displays desirable traits such as maturity, friendliness, approachability and a sense of humour. The successful candidate would also need to have the ability to remain calm and level headed in emergency situations and be totally flexible about working with new people, flying different routes and working unsociable hours.

What do you think the role of cabin crew involves/What do you think is the primary responsibility of Cabin Crew?

Cabin crew are on board an aircraft for safety reasons. In the event of a real life emergency, the cabin crew must ensure that passengers follow the captains instructions, use safety equipment correctly and stay as calm as possible.

During the flight, the cabin crew spend a lot of time looking after the comfort of passengers. This involves giving special attention to children travelling alone, disabled people or people who are ill. Crew must appear friendly and sympathetic to anyone needing help, advice, reassurance, sympathy or even, at times, firm persuasion.

Other duties during the flight include preparing and serving meals and drinks and clearing up afterwards, selling duty free goods, and helping passengers to use in-flight entertainment systems. There is also paperwork to complete, this can include flight reports, customs and immigration documents, accounts of duty free sales and meal and drink orders.

At the end of the flight, the crew make sure the passengers leave the aircraft safely.

What qualities do you have that you feel would make you a good cabin crew member?

My skills and experience closely matches the major requirements and diverse responsibilities for this role. Plus I will bring a depth of practical knowledge and experience that will transfer well and benefit my performance as a cabin crew member.

I am used to working under pressure and to tight time scales and I thrive on the challenges that these situations create.

Furthermore, I am an experienced team player and always work hard to support and contribute towards the overall team goal for success. I am a people person and would consistently deliver excellent customer service to passengers of all levels and I'm driven to achieve, to surpass my most recent record, so you'll never see me deliver merely acceptable performance.

I feel that both my personal qualities and the skills and experience I have gained from working in client-facing roles for the past 8 years would make an excellent member of Cabin Crew.

Are you willing to start as a trainee?
Yes, definitely. This is a new area for me, and I believe in getting a good foundation in the basics before progressing. An entry level position will enable me to learn the business inside out, and will give me the opportunity to grow when I prove myself. I also have a great deal of knowledge and work experience, which I'm sure, will contribute to my rapid progress through training. I am sure I shall learn quickly and I see it as a really exciting opportunity.

Do you know anything about Cabin Crew training?
The training lasts for 5 weeks, and subjects covered include: Safety and emergency procedures, such as fire fighting, first aid, security and hijack procedures, and crowd control. Also covered is dealing with passengers and foreign currency and personal grooming and deportment. This initial period is followed by further on-the-job training, and usually a period of regular on board assessment.

What qualities do you think a good Cabin Crew member should have/What do you think it takes to be a successful cabin crew member/How many of those qualities do you have?
Passengers generally spend more time with the cabin crew than with any other members of the airlines staff, so they have a vital role in giving a good impression of the airline as a whole. This means cabin crew members need to have good communication and customer care skills and display desirable traits such as sincerity, a spirit of enthusiasm, confidence and a sense of humour.

They must be totally flexible about working with new people, flying different routes and working unsociable hours. They may deal with money, including foreign currency, so they should be honest as well as confident with numbers. Team working skills are also very important as is being fairly self contained, and satisfied in your own company.

The ability to manage change and adversity is another necessary quality for cabin crew. They should be able to show that they have strength of character to cope, which means approaching difficult and emergency situations in a calm and objective way – and being polite yet resolute in handling an abrasive customer.

These are all attributes that I possess and is the primary reason why I will make an excellent member of cabin crew.

How do you feel about the 6 month probationary period?
I can see no problem with a probationary period. I am a fast learner and it shouldn't take me long to prove myself.

Do you think the role of cabin crew is glamorous?
Well, it certainly is perceived as glamorous and it certainly has its benefits of travel. People see cabin crew in action, jetting around the world and form an immediate impression of what they think the job involves. In fact, the customer sees only a fraction of what goes on in order to make each flight a success. The truth is, cabin crew have to combine working as a flying waiter or waitress, mobile shop assistant, cleaner, plus all the emergency services rolled into one. It can be an exhausting and disorientating lifestyle that places tough demands on family and social commitments.

Therefore, no, I don't see the position of cabin crew as a glamorous role but rather a challenging role.

What do you think are the disadvantages of this position/How will you cope with the disadvantages/ What problems do you think you'll face in this job?
Having thoroughly researched this position, I expect that this job will present the usual risks that present other travellers, such as theft of personal belongings, bites and stings from insects, jet lag and service disruptions, to name but a few issues. However, I have considered these issues before I applied and will be sure to take any preventative measures necessary, such as carrying travellers cheques or bank card rather than lots of cash, using an insecticide or other similar product and in the case of jet lag, control food and water intake before the flight and get plenty of sleep.

So by being aware of these issues, they appear to be minor issues rather than disadvantages.

Extras to remember
Some would think that working different shifts would be a disadvantage; however, I enjoy a variable schedule.

I relish a challenge and there's nothing that I've seen in this job that intimidates me in any way.

What do you think are the advantages of the position?

Working as a Cabin Crew member is not just a job, but a way of life and provides an alternative and very stimulating lifestyle where no two working days are likely to be the same. The sheer dynamics of different crew, passenger profiles, destinations and roster structures ensure that there will always be variety.

Furthermore, there are opportunities to visit places and experience cultures that are beyond most peoples reach. Cabin crew go to places they always dreamed of and find interest in destinations they would not necessarily have chosen to go to.

Additionally, it is a good feeling to deliver businessmen to their meetings on time, reunite family and friends; deliver newly weds to their honeymoon destinations, or vacationers to their dream holiday place. There is genuine feeling of doing something worthwhile, in a unique way which not many jobs regularly produce at the end of a hard day.

Will you be able to cope with the change in environment?

Definitely; I welcome the challenge of learning about and adapting to a new environment, that's one of the reasons I'm seeking to make a career change right now. Any major change, while always containing some challenge, is a chance to grow, learn, and advance.

What do you expect from this job?

I expect that the role will provide an alternative and very stimulating lifestyle where no two working days are the same. The sheer dynamics of different crew, passenger profiles, destinations and roster structures ensure that there will always be variety. It's a job I will find very rewarding in a number of ways.

What will you look forward to most in this job?

The opportunity to build a career with an established airline with a good reputation; the chance to work as part of a team and do something important that gives me satisfaction. I could use the skills I have developed and be sufficiently challenged to develop whilst learning from new people, processes and clients. I could then look forward to opportunities my success in this role would bring.

If you could, what would you change about this position?

I relish the challenges that this position will provide and there's nothing I've seen that intimidates me in any way. By applying for this position, I have accepted everything that comes with it and therefore I would not change anything.

If pressed further mention turbulence.

Why should we hire you instead of someone with prior Cabin Crew experience?
Although I might not have previous cabin crew experience, I have the necessary skills to make an impressive start and the willingness to learn and improve. Sometimes employers can do better when they hire people who don't have a great deal of repetitive experience. That way, they can train these employees in their methods and ways of doing the job. Training is much easier than un-training.

Or

I may not have had many years of experience in this field, but my knowledge and ability to learn quickly and work hard will enable me to make an immediate contribution to the job. With some specialised training and my desire to learn and improve myself, I could accomplish a lot in this position.

Why should we hire you for this position rather than another applicant/I have a preferred candidate for this role, change my mind.
I can't tell you why you should hire me instead of another candidate but, I can tell you why you should hire me.

Why should we hire you?
This job is exactly what I'm looking for, and I'm exactly what you are wanting. My skills and experience closely matches the major requirements and diverse responsibilities for this role. Plus I will bring a depth of practical knowledge and experience that will transfer well and benefit my performance as a cabin crew member, such as handling customer service issues, sales, working under pressure and communicating with different types of people.

Furthermore, I am an honest and upright person, who understands the need for high standards and rules. I refuse to compromise on standards and integrity. Within this, I can be relied upon to put the customer first and will always consider the needs of colleagues and of the organisation.

I'm driven to achieve, to surpass my most recent record, so you'll never see me deliver merely acceptable performance. I keep calm and don't let attention to detail slip when there is a lot of pressure and can be relied on to pull with the team when it's facing any kind of challenge.

I really think that the position could use someone with my attributes. XYZ Airlines provide a fine service. I can offer top professionalism. Together we will make a winning team.

What challenges do you look forward to?
An opportunity to apply my interpersonal skills in a new team, with a different set of customers and in a different environment.

What do you hope to achieve from this position/What do you wish to gain at XYZ airlines?
I'd like to transfer all I've experienced to this airline, while at the same time having the opportunity to meet new challenges and achieve new goals.

How is your work experience related to Cabin Crew/How has your work experience prepared you for the role?
My work experience closely matches the requirements and diverse responsibilities of this position in many ways. For example,

Working as a hairdresser, I interact with a range of people on a daily basis and have to handle responsibility with a minimum of supervision. I am responsible for establishing_and maintaining relationships with clients, dealing with customer service issues, sales, and admin. Furthermore, I am required to stand for long periods, work unsociable hours, pay attention to detail and be self starting with a lot of mental discipline.

My experience, I feel, will transfer well and enable me to make a significant contribution to this position and coupled with the training I will receive, I believe I will make an outstanding employee.

What makes this job different from your current/previous ones/ What was the least relevant job you have held?
I really don't believe any two jobs are exactly the same, different customers, different projects and different approaches. However, there are more similarities than differences and if I focus on the similarities rather than the differences I will accomplish more and be contributing right from the start.

What is it about being a Cabin Crew member that you think you do not presently have?

From what I know about the position, I seem to have all the skills and experience required to make a thorough success. I don't believe that there are any areas that indicate gaps in my ability to do this job well and any gaps that may exist will be presented and filled during the 5 weeks training.

Do you feel ready for a more responsible position/In what ways has your work experience prepared you to take on greater responsibility?

As I manage a business with real success I can certainly demonstrate that I can manage responsibility. I believe that 6 years experience working closely with customers, has prepared me professionally and personally to move up to this role. My customer care and teamwork skills have been finely tuned over the years and I know I am capable of greater achievements, which is why I'm interviewing for this position.

Do you feel confident in your ability to handle this position?

Absolutely, I'm very confident in my abilities. I'm familiar with the basic job requirements and I learn quickly. It undoubtedly will take time and effort on my part, but I'm more than willing to devote that time and effort.

What challenges do you anticipate from this position?

An opportunity to apply my interpersonal skills in a new team, with a different set of customers and in a different environment; the challenge will come from all those things.

Do you think your lack of language skills will affect your ability to perform the job?

I admit my language skills are a little light. However, should I be offered the position, I would be sure to increase my language abilities; I have a basic knowledge and understanding of conversational French, and would welcome the opportunity to further increase my fluency. I am also presently learning Spanish.

What would you bring to the position//In what ways will XYZ airlines benefit from hiring you//I'm not sure you are suitable for the position, convince me.

XYZ Airlines would be getting someone whose skills and experience closely matches the major requirements and diverse responsibilities for this role. Plus I will bring a depth of practical knowledge and experience that will transfer well and benefit my performance as a cabin crew member, such as handling customer service issues, sales, working under pressure and communicating with different types of people.

Furthermore, I'm driven to achieve, to surpass my most recent record, so you'll never see me deliver merely acceptable performance. I am a hardworking member of the team and I keep calm and don't let attention to detail slip when there is a lot of pressure.

I have an outgoing personality and I pride myself on being able to build rapport quickly with new people. In fact, at Any Hair Salon, I was often asked to carry out the shampoo because the manager knew I would make the client feel welcome and important.

I really think that the position could use someone with my attributes. XYZ Airlines provide a fine service. I can offer top professionalism. Together we will make a winning team.

Wouldn't you miss spending time with your family and friends on these special occasions?

Naturally, I would miss spending time with my friends and family on these occasions, but my job and my career are as equally important to me as my friends and family and my family and friends respect that fact. Technology has made it possible for everyone to communicate easier which also helps.

How do you feel about working at Christmas, and other special occasions?

I understand this from your job description and I considered this issue carefully before I applied, so it would not be a problem at all, I would be quite prepared to undertake this work when it is necessary.

This is a long hours culture, is that a problem for you?

I understand that this a demanding job that I am applying for, but I really do thrive on the challenge of this sort of work and have worked long hours in the past– so I am willing to work whatever hours are necessary to get the work done.

Have you worked on night shifts before?
So far I haven't worked on a night shift. However, I have often worked long hours and evening shifts, so I could work a night shift without any problems.

How do you feel about living out of a suitcase?
I don't have any concerns; I was aware of this fact before I applied for this position.

How do you feel about a formal dress code?
I have always liked to dress formally and feel very comfortable wearing suits. I realise that a standard of dress is necessary in order to project a positive image to the customers and general public.

How will you cope with the wide range of ethnic differences/How do you feel about working in a very multi-cultural environment, colleagues and customers?
I learnt about different cultures, customs and religions from a young age, through my years of education at school. I also have a cosmopolitan group of friends, so I feel comfortable with people who are from different ethnic backgrounds.

Any Hair Salon specialised in Afro Caribbean hairdressing and therefore attracted a large variety of people from many ethnic backgrounds. The manager and supervisor were both originally from Jamaica and spoke English as a second language. Not only did I have a good working relationship with them, we also became good friends.

These experiences will help me deal with all the different cultures I will encounter on a daily basis. If I am offered the position, I will also take steps towards enhancing my language skills to allow more flexibility.

How will you adapt your behaviour to the wide range of ethnic differences?
I will be careful about body language and gestures to ensure there are no misunderstandings, due to differentiations in meanings to different cultures.

If a language barrier exists, I will try to ensure that the passenger can understand my style of speech (pace, vocabulary or accent), by speaking slightly slower than usual, with clearer pronunciations. I will be careful to avoid slang, jargon, buzzwords, clichés, and colloquialisms and to further ensure that the passenger understands I will make more use of facial expressions and hand gestures.

I never assume that they understand, I check for signs indicating a lack of comprehension, such as a vague or quizzical expression on the client's face, and a lack of response. If I feel that the client has not understood what I am trying to say, I am prepared to spend a little time to discuss it with them.

If I am offered the position, I will also take steps towards enhancing my language skills to allow more flexibility.

What contribution can you make to ensure passengers will fly with us again?
Service with a smile and a friendly, positive attitude will keep them loyal and keep them coming back.

A positive attitude to my work will not only ensure that the passengers enjoy their time with us; it will also help me by making my job easier, more interesting, more enjoyable and more rewarding.

GENERAL PERCEPTIONS

What is your idea of success/Define a successful career?
Success for me is about knowing that I have made a difference both to myself and my organisation. I like to make a difference to myself by developing my own skills. And I like to make a difference to my organisation by achieving good results.

Or

If I am successful, I will meet each new challenge with the confidence in my ability, yet will continue to be given new challenges that develop my abilities and make me even more productive.

Has anyone in the business world ever been an inspiration to you/Who was the most influential person in your life?

Yes, several people. During my working life, I have been fortunate to have worked with some very skilled people who were exceptionally good at certain aspects of their role and who have influenced me. Through observation and discussion, I have identified what made them good at what they do and have tried to follow their examples. I think I've learned an even greater amount from these individuals than from text books I've read and the courses I've taken?

I have been most influenced by my manager at Any Hair Salon. From the time I began working at the salon, she took a sincere interest in my work and under her guidance, I grew personally and professionally. She expected a lot from me but gave a lot in return. She taught me many necessary skills and work methods and provided constant motivation and encouragement for my efforts. We always felt mutual respect and trust for each other. I consider myself very fortunate to have had her by my side early in my career, as a supervisor, teacher and remarkable person. She served as a role model for me and helped me develop my leadership and interpersonal skills.

When answering these questions, it is important to bear in mind that there is a big difference between just delivering a product, and providing customer service. Successful candidates are likely to be those who understand that 'service' starts before boarding and ends after disembarkation. Candidates who think that the work ends once the last meal tray has been collected in will not progress very far!

How would you define good customer service?

Good customer service is: Customer needs and expectations being met all of the time, every time throughout the life of the product or service. Without this, you have no customer loyalty.

What is the key to providing good customer service?

Good customer care is about making people feel secure, relaxed and valued. This can be achieved by being friendly and approachable when accommodating the various needs of the customer, while showing empathy and interest.

When have you witnessed poor customer service/When have you witnessed good customer service?

I needed a particular material for a dress I was making. In most stores the salesperson would give me a quick 'no' before I finished explaining what I was looking for. Then in one store, I found a lady who waited patiently, giving me her undivided attention while I finished telling her what I wanted. She looked at me with a pleasant countenance, while she proceeded to explain why she didn't have the material I was asking for. She also made some helpful suggestions. As I looked at her, while she was talking to me, there was such sorrow in her voice that I actually began to feel sorry for the poor lady because she didn't have the material to sell me.

I didn't realise that she was taking it so seriously until I began to get sorry for her. I vowed, the next time I needed haberdashery supplies I would surely look to that lady.

What do you think constitutes poor customer service?

Major factors that contribute to poor customer service include job not done right, too slow, lack of courtesy, indifferent and unqualified personnel.

When have you provided good customer service?

I provide good customer service every day; it is a necessary part of my job to ensure clients return. I take great pride in providing the best service I possibly can, and have never received any negative feedback.

A time when I have been particularly happy with the customer service I provided was when I was working at Any Hair Salon. I was in the staff room during my lunch break and I could hear a lot of noise coming from inside the salon. I went out to see what was happening and there were two young children who were there whilst their mum was having her hair done. The children were bored and not very happy; they were running around and constantly tugging at their mums coat asking to go home. I could sense that the situation was causing an inconvenience for not only the client but also the stylist.

I decided to go over and try to keep the children occupied. I sat them down and asked them if they would like to have their hair plaited. Their eyes lit up and they jumped at the chance. After finishing their hair, we sat down and made shiny bead bracelets from some hair beads. We had lots of fun and they really enjoyed themselves, which resulted in the client and the hair stylist having a stress free time.

The client was very thankful for my effort which was very rewarding. I felt really pleased that with just a little extra effort, I had made such a difference.

When have you thought that your customer service could have been better?

I provide good customer service every day; it is a necessary part of my job to ensure clients return. I take great pride in providing the best service I possibly can, and have never received any negative feedback.

Not matter how much you are probed, do not give in.

What do you find most challenging about providing customer service?

The most challenging aspect is trying to keep everybody happy, the customer as well as the company. I enjoy the challenges of providing customer care. I think it's something I'm good at.

What do you most/least enjoy about providing customer care?
The most enjoyable aspect I would have to say is that because I genuinely care about my client's satisfaction, it rewards me personally when I know that they are happy with the job I did, which in turn drives me to do better.

The least enjoyable aspect is when you have bent over backwards to provide good customer service, and nothing you do satisfies the customer. There are two sides to every situation so I take the rough with the smooth and make the best of each circumstance.

What do you think is the main cause of some passenger's frustrations?
Common causes of irritation for passengers include flight delays, lost luggage, inadequate catering facilities and lack of space. Other causes may include incorrect, poorly displayed or missing information and poor service.

What aspects of customer service are most important to our passengers?
People will return to a favourite airline not merely because the price, destinations, in-flight entertainment and food is good. Equally differential in their choice is the standard of service – passengers want to feel welcome, be entertained and amused while being looked after well and safely – whatever their needs, by people who are friendly, polite, approachable, willing to listen and professional, whatever the time of day and whatever the pressure.

Or

Anybody can fly you from A to B – that is the core product – but the standards of service, food and in-flight entertainment are vitally important, because, next to price, they are the main reason why customers make the choice they do.

Why do you think some passengers take out their frustrations on Cabin Crew?
Cabin Crew wear the airlines uniform, and are therefore considered representative. This makes them a target for passengers to vent their frustrations upon.

How are you going to cope/How do you think this will make you feel?
I simply see it as part of the work. I will not take it personally because I know I am doing my job. I will remain calm, be professional and continue to offer the best service I can.

Do you think the customer is always right?
It depends on the situation. Whilst every customer is important, those who exhibit abusive behaviour or do anything to compromise safety are straying beyond the boundary. Therefore, the customer isn't always right.

How would you deal with a passenger who is not right but believes he is right?
I would explain the company's rules and policies to the passenger in a calm, professional and positive manner. Hopefully, this should clarify any misconceptions that the passenger may have.

How would you define teamwork?
The idea of teamwork is that a group of people who work in a coordinated way should be able to complete most tasks better and more effectively than the same group of people acting individually.

What do you think makes a crew work well together?
Essentially, a crew works well together when there is strong team commitment, open communication and good leadership.
They have respect for each other and the organisation they are part of, feelings are expressed freely and conflict is faced up and worked through.

Additionally, a team works well together when their intellectual and practical capabilities are challenged and put to the test, and some pressure is present. That gives them a sense of urgency of the job and stretches their faculties to the limit.

When all the above elements are met, it creates a feeling of camaraderie, and sometimes the team are able to inspire and motivate each other beyond even their own expectations.

What do you think prevents a crew working well together?
Teams may break down because lack of communication or poor leadership, or the root cause might be something relatively trivial like, clash of personalities, lack of motivation, and trust and sometimes training or ability is insufficient for the task.

Should any of these situations occur, how would or have you dealt with the problem?
If there is lack of communication or leadership, I will take the initiative. If the problem is down to clash of personalities, I would act as a mediator, bringing the colleagues together and openly discussing the issue. It is very important for me to preserve neutrality, maintain integrity and project sincerity in those circumstances. If there is lack of motivation, I would challenge them to get something worthwhile done and nine times out of ten they will do it, and lack of training would require more training.

Are you a good team player?

Yes I do consider myself a good team player because I am self motivated, I respect other people's opinions, I communicate well with my colleagues and I can be relied on to pull with the team.

What is your definition of a good employee?

A good employee assumes responsibility, always works to the best of their abilities and is interested in improving. They communicate well and appropriately, feel and show team spirit, appreciate differences and show respect for others. They are also reliable and trustworthy and can appreciate criticism – not just tolerate or accept it, but benefit from it.

What do you enjoy most about working as part of a team?

The joy of working harmoniously with a group of people who are dedicated to something bigger than themselves, and are completely loyal to each other, counts in my experience as one of the most rewarding things in life. A new dimension is created when people work harmoniously together.

Nobody's perfect, but a team can be.

What do you least enjoy about working as part of a team?

People not pulling their weight, is the least enjoyable aspect of working in a team, however I've noticed that such people simply lack enthusiasm and confidence, and that energetic and cheerful co workers can often change that, because enthusiasm is contagious.

What do you find most challenging about being part of a team?

The most challenging aspect is inspiring and motivating other team members. Each has different needs and is motivated by different things.

What role would you usually assume in a team situation/Are you a leader or follower? Why?

I am both a leader and follower, if a situation comes up and someone has to take charge and I feel I can, then I will, but if a situation comes up and someone else has already taken charge and is solving it, I will follow. I am whatever I need to be.

What do you expect from your colleagues?
I expect from my colleagues what I expect from myself.

To value their own contribution, but not to the extent that it becomes more important than achieving the team objective, to be hard working, focused on quality customer care, honest and someone that others can rely upon.

What do you expect from your superiors?
I believe superiors should practice good management, lead by example and act as a positive role model. In addition, they should be secure in their ability to train, motivate, encourage and lead others.

How will you react if your colleagues or superiors do not match up to your expectations?
I would be very surprised if my expectations are not met because the criteria of people XYZ Airlines look for. If it does occur however, I will not, under any circumstances, let it affect my professionalism or desire to do my best.

Or

I accept that my personal standards will sometimes be compromised, but they will not be permanently affected by the influence of others, or by circumstances, and I will still continue to do my best for the benefit of the passengers.

What do you think your colleagues expect of you?
What I expect from my colleagues, they should and probably do expect from me.

To value my own contribution, but not to the extent that it becomes more important than achieving the team objective, to be hard working, focused on quality customer care, honest and someone that others can rely upon.

What kind of supervisor do you like to work with/around?
I enjoy working for anyone who practices good management and knows how to tap the potential of team members. The kinds who trust themselves and their employees to carry out their responsibilities – supervisors, who are secure in their ability to train, motivate, encourage and lead others. If the right employees are there, they will respond favourably. The result is a mature relationship with mutual respect where everyone succeeds and the company prospers.

What qualities or behaviour do you least like in a boss/leader/What kind of supervisor do you not like to work with/around?
Although I can work with any leader, I would prefer to work with superiors who do not exhibit tendencies such as impatience, panic or being hypercritical.

How will you cope if a crew member in charge has some of the qualities/behaviours you dislike?
I accept that my personal standards will sometimes be compromised, and I will not, under any circumstances, let it affect my professionalism or desire to do my best.

However, if their behaviour interferes with my work, the first thing I do is watch and take notice if I've seen the behaviour in three other situations with the person. The reason for this is because the first two times are possibly chance but by the third time it's probably a pattern.

The second thing I would do is notice whether or not this person is dealing with a lot of stress. Stress may be causing this adverse behaviour and is not a regular occurrence.

The third thing to do is to ask myself if I've been suffering from any exceptional stress. Stress on me may be causing me to see the world in a way that is contrary to what is actually going on.

The fourth: have I had an adult-to-adult conversation with this person? There are many times when the other person may or may not know that his/her behaviour is causing a problem for you and talking to him or her can clear up what turns out to be a simple misunderstanding.

If that does nothing and the situation continues or worsens, I may then seek guidance from a higher source.

In your opinion, what makes the best leader?

In my opinion, the best leader is skilled in the art of communication and is very much a people person who encourages cooperation between staff and acts decisively in a crisis or under pressure.

They act as a role model for the team members, by acting professionally at all times and maintaining standards by supporting the company's procedures and activities.

They have a keen sense of what is fair and deal with all people equally and justly.

What qualities do you admire in a good leader?

I admire any leader who leads by example and acts as a positive role model for the team members. A leader who encourages cooperation between staff, acts decisively in a crisis or under pressure and has the ability to motivate and inspire confidence in others. These types of leaders usually win the confidence and respect of the entire team.

Other admirable attributes include: Recognising, using and showing appreciation for the skills of individual team members, accepting responsibility when things go wrong, duplicating skills in others, embracing both leader and follower and delegating while maintaining control.

What minimum quality should a person have to be your team-mate?

Although I can work with any person, I prefer to work with people who are honest because dishonest people are hard to trust and rely on.

How will you react if you do end up working with someone who is dishonest?

I wouldn't let their actions prevent me from doing my best but, obviously I couldn't support a colleague who was behaving dishonestly either toward the company or with a customer.

How would you define a good working relationship?

A good working relationship combines fairness, mutual respect and trust, openness and honesty in communication.

It is important that there is enough empathy and warmness towards colleagues but you should maintain just enough distance to be able to deal with problems that arise without being hampered by personal feelings.

What do you think is an ideal working environment?
The ideal work environment is a harmonious one, where team members work together towards a common goal and concentrate their efforts to get the job done in the shortest possible time. Their intellectual and practical capabilities are challenged and put to the test, and some pressure is present. That gives them a sense of urgency of the job and stretches their faculties to the limit. They have all equipment necessary to do the job, and undivided support from their superiors. That is the environment in which people improve in their jobs and achieve tangible results.

How would you react if the ideal working environment is not present?
No work environment is 100% perfect and to everyone's liking, so I would adapt and make the best of what I have.

Do you feel a supervisor and employee should have a strictly business relationship?
Socialising on one's own time depends on company policy and individual case.

My philosophy is that business and pleasure can be combined, but you have to set limits. There's a definite difference between being friendly with your co workers and working with friends. It's important to maintain just enough distance to be able to deal with problems that arise without being hampered by personal feelings. At work, there should always be a professional relationship in force.

Has your social life ever involved associates or co workers?
Some of my closest friends are also my ex co workers. We share the same interests and a similar lifestyle and feel close to each other, probably because of the close and productive relationships we had at work.

How did you manage to maintain enough distance with your colleagues at Any Hair Salon?
At work, we always had a professional working relationship and worked well together.

What would you say about a supervisor who is unfair and difficult to work with?

The first thing I do is watch and take notice if I've seen the behaviour in three other situations with the superior. The reason for this is because the first two times are probably by chance, but by the third time it's probably a pattern.

The second thing I would do is notice whether or not this person is dealing with a lot of stress. Stress may be causing this adverse behaviour and is not a regular occurrence.

The third thing to do is to ask myself if I've been suffering from any exceptional stress. Stress on me may be causing me to see the world in a way that is contrary to what is actually going on.

The fourth: I would make an appointment to see the supervisor and have an adult to adult conversation. There are many times when the person may or may not know that his/her behaviour is causing a problem for you and talking to him or her can clear up what turns out to be a simple misunderstanding.

How would you approach this adult to adult conversation?

I would enter the discussion in the frame of mind that we were equally responsible for whatever problems existed, and that this wasn't just the supervisor's problem. I would diplomatically explain that I feel uncomfortable in our professional relationship, that I feel he or she is not treating me as a professional, and therefore that I might not be performing up to standard in some way – I would ask for his or her input as to what I must do to create a professional relationship.

How do you show respect for your superiors?

Respect is very important to me. As an employee, I try to respect my superiors not only by following their guidance, but also seeking their guidance. When a trusting relationship is formed, I have often found that my superiors have appreciated concerns or opinions that I have raised to them. There is mutual respect.

How would you define a Conductive Work Atmosphere?

A conductive work atmosphere is a harmonious one, where the team has a genuine interest in its work and desire to deliver a good service.

How do you deal with authority?

I have no problems at all with authority. I like to know what my reporting line is and I realise that a big part of my job is satisfying the demands my superiors will make upon me.

Do you criticise others/under what circumstances?

I don't really criticise, because I don't feel it is a constructive way to approach others, but I do try to offer constructive feedback. The circumstances would involve, when the objectives are not being met.

How do you criticise others?

I'm careful how I express my opinions; I never criticise in open forum. I gather my thoughts and formulate my ideas and then present them to the other person privately, that way you avoid belittling the other person.

I ensure the conversation focuses on any business discrepancies and does not get personal or spiral into blaming others. I also ensure that all feedback I give is as positive as possible so that the person on the receiving end thinks that any bad messages are balanced by their positive attributes and I always finish the conversation on a positive note.

What if your opinions are sought in open forum? i.e. a meeting?

If opinions are sought in a meeting, I will give mine, although I am careful to be aware of others feelings.

How would you handle a team member or senior crew who makes a mistake and does not take criticism?

To soften the message, without losing its impact, I try to ensure that all feedback is as positive as possible. By ensuring that all feedback is as positive as possible, the person on the receiving end thinks that any bad messages are balanced by their positive attributes. It's much more likely that the feedback will be accepted – and appreciated that way.

Do you speak up if your opinion differs from that of others?

If my opinion differs from others, I put myself into their shoes and try to see it. Then I explain my opinions to them. In that process, the right solution is almost always found.

What action do you take if you disagree with the decision of your manager?
I would speak up. But there are times when tact is required – for example, if my manager were to say something in a meeting that I felt was wrong, I would wait until we had a moment alone to put my opinion across. At the end of the day though, I recognise that a manager is entitled to make decisions that I may not agree with. As long as I feel that I have been given a fair chance to air my views, I would have to go along with their decisions.

Do you try hard to get people (colleagues) to like you?
It is in my nature to try to get on with everyone I work with and I input a lot of effort into building trustworthy business relationships. If someone doesn't like me, I will see if there is anything I can do to change their perspective, but if I cannot, I will try to at least gain their respect so that we can continue to have a professional working relationship, where personal feelings do not interfere with the work.

Or

Good working relationships are essential to a successful career and to getting the work done, so I always try to earn the respect of others. If someone doesn't like me, I will see if there is anything I can do to change their perspective, but if I cannot, I will try to at least gain their respect so that we can continue to have a professional working relationship, where personal feelings do not interfere with the work.

How would you try to change their perspective/gain their respect?
By continuing to be respectful and professional towards the other person, I would hope to change their perspective and/or establish their respect.

How important to you is the aim to build relationships with clients, co-workers, peers and management?
To me, interaction between people is the most important factor in any business. The ability to work together as a team, absolute honesty with peers and customers, and a mutual feeling of trust and understanding, are essential for creating an efficient environment.

Have you successfully worked with a difficult co worker?
If by difficult you mean a person who is constantly complaining then yes I have; I remember one member of staff was always complaining, nothing was ever good enough or couldn't possibly work. Everyone had lost patience with her, but because she was so incredibly sensitive and really good at her job, no one said anything.

I spent some time with her and tactfully told her that it appeared as if she was always putting our ideas down. On hearing the feedback, she was genuinely horrified at her own behaviour. She explained that she hadn't realised it had made everyone feel that way and agreed that from then on, she would try to be more positive. Very quickly after that, we saw a change in her behaviour. She became more conscious of her own behaviour, deliberately trying to be more considerate. And from that point on, no one could have hoped for a more committed team member.

Have you ever had difficulties getting along with others/Tell us about someone you haven't got on with/How did you deal with the situation?
I got on well with all my colleagues at Any Hair Salon. Naturally I was closer to some of my colleagues than with others, but we all got on well and worked well as a team.

Or

I remember one co-worker in particular who flat out didn't like me, it didn't matter what I did or said, or whether I tried to avoid or befriend this person. After a couple of days of subtle hostility, I decided to assert myself. I diplomatically explained that I acknowledged their personal dislike for me and drew upon the fact that we are both talented, dedicated and hardworking individuals and can therefore put aside our differences for the good of the salon, I asked for input as to what I must do to create a professional relationship. Although we never became friends, I was thereafter able to have pleasant exchanges with the person. I had bonded us in a novel way, under less than ideal circumstances.

What would you do if no amount of effort on your part solved the problem?
I would maintain cordial relations, but not go out of my way to seek more than a business like acquaintance. If nothing else, I always try to keep the channels of communication open by talking. Not speaking will not move either of us any further forward.

Do you prefer to work alone or as part of a team/ Do you like to work in a team?
I am equally happy working alone or as part of a team and I am equally efficient in both. However, I prefer team spirit and the interactions between team members while working towards a common goal. In a team, people learn from each other and tend to achieve results faster, more efficiently and with greater satisfaction. The team approach to problem solving creates a harmonized work force and a more productive environment.

Or

Whilst I enjoy working in a team, I can work just as well and as hard alone. Though more pressure to produce might exist, it also proves to be a challenge.

Or

Whether I prefer to work as part of a team or alone depend on the best way to complete the job. Either way, I would work equally hard with the initiative required for success.

Do you like to work with people?
Yes. I have always enjoyed the teamwork and interaction with my co-workers and customers.

Describe your ideal work group.
My ideal work group would be one which has an infusion of character among the participants, where the members are able to inspire and motivate each other while retaining mutual trust and respect. There is open communication and good leadership and everyone is motivated to achieve a common aim. Decisions are made by consensus, feelings are expressed freely and conflict is faced up and worked through.

However, I understand that no work group is 100% perfect and to everyone's liking, so I adapt and make the best of what I have, while continuing to do my best for the benefit of the customers.

Name three adjectives that best describe your ideal work colleague/What would you look for in a colleague?
It's difficult to think of an 'ideal' work colleague, however if I had to choose three adjectives I'd say: Communicative, honest and dependable.

What types of people do you work well with/around/What types of people do you like to work with/around?
I'd like to think I work well with most people, however, I prefer to work with people who can communicate effectively, are honest, dependable and nice in behaviour.

What types of people are you most comfortable with?
I am most comfortable with people who are honest, because dishonest people are hard to trust and rely on.

How will you react if you do end up working with someone who is dishonest?
I wouldn't allow their behaviour to affect the way I work, but obviously I couldn't support a colleague who was behaving dishonestly either toward the company or with a client.

What types of people do you not like to work with/around?
I would say that I don't particularly enjoy working with people who display aggressive behaviour. People who are aggressive are often competitive; their goal is to win, which means that somebody else has to lose. This may be achieved by putting others down by overriding their feelings. Aggressive people attack as an immediate form of response; they often over react and in doing so hurt or humiliate the individuals they are dealing with.

But at the end of the day, it doesn't matter if I do not like who I work with, as long as the team objectives are met. I do not, under any circumstances, let it affect my professionalism or desire to do my best.

What types of people do you find it difficult to work with/around?
If I had to pick a type I find difficult, it would be people who use aggressive behaviour. The aggressive person expresses his or her feelings, needs and ideas at the expense of others. Aggressive people attack as an immediate form of response; they often over react and in doing so hurt or humiliate the individuals they are dealing with.

But at the end of the day, it doesn't matter if I do not like who I work with, as long as the team objectives are met. I do not, under any circumstances, let it affect my professionalism or desire to do my best.

What behaviour of a person do you not like/Tell us about someone you dislike?
I do not like aggressive behaviour. The aggressor may shout at the people who fail to do all they demand, or it may be indirect and subversive, such as slipping in occasional put-downs until they rob people of their self confidence. They are both deadly and they are both bad behaviour.

But at the end of the day, it doesn't matter if I do not like who I work with, as long as the team objectives are met. I do not, under any circumstances, let it affect my professionalism or desire to do my best.

How will you deal with someone who possesses this aggressive behaviour?
I would have an adult-to-adult conversation with the person. There are many times when the other person may or may not know that his/her behaviour is causing a problem and talking to him or her can clear up what turns out to be a simple misunderstanding.

If after the discussion, the behaviour continues or worsens, I will seek guidance and support from a superior in dealing with the situation.

How would you approach the conversation?
I would approach the conversation in a calm, assertive and objective manner.

What types of people try your patience?
Not much makes me impatient, however I understand that situations can occur occasionally, but instead of getting impatient, I exert my energy into maintaining my professional approach and conduct.

What types of people annoy you?
Usually I am not affected by annoying people. However I understand that situations can occur occasionally, but instead of getting annoyed, I exert my energy into maintaining my professional approach and conduct.

Do you have difficulties tolerating people with different views or interests than you?
No. I don't let the different views or interests of others affect how I feel about them. I judge them by the quality and quantity of their work. I get along with anyone whose accomplishments I can respect. Differing views and personalities add richness to a team; after all you don't want a team of clones.

This job will require you to work with people from very different backgrounds to yourself – how will you cope?

I worked with people from different backgrounds while I was working at Any Hair Salon. Both the manager and supervisor were originally from Jamaica and spoke English as a second language and many of my other colleagues were much more highly qualified than myself, but not only did I have a good working relationship with these people, we also became good friends.

Based on this past experience, I believe I will cope fine.

How will you cope with the wide range of personalities among our employees?

The same way I have coped in the past. Working at Any Hair Salon, I worked with people who had very different personalities. Some of them had loud, exuberant personalities whilst others were sensitive and quiet. I understand that a range of personalities exist in any workplace and I observe and respect each of them accordingly.

Do you think you can get along with X personality?

I don't let the personalities of others affect how I feel about them. I judge them by the quality and quantity of their work. I get along with anyone whose accomplishments I can respect.

How do you get along with different kinds of people?

Dealing with people is something I really enjoy. I like contact with colleagues and clients and would generally describe myself as a sociable person. I have very good interpersonal skills and I pride myself on being able to build rapport quickly with new people. To me, establishing rapport seems to be a natural tendency. In fact, at Any Hair Salon, I was often asked to carry out the shampoo because the manager knew I would make the clients feel welcome and important.

How do you make clients feel welcome and important?

I make them feel welcome and important by making them feel comfortable, relaxed and valued.

What is most important in the workplace, total honesty, or supportiveness towards colleagues?

I think honesty and supportiveness are both important, but obviously I couldn't support a colleague who was behaving dishonestly either toward the company or with a client.

How do you show interest in your co workers/How do you go about establishing rapport and trust/How will you establish a working relationship with our employees?

To me, establishing rapport seems to be a natural tendency. The greatest part is often established non-verbally. By being empathetic, treating people with respect and being willing to listen and help, I create a feeling of trust and confidence in my team mates.

Matching my behaviour to suit the particular situation or person also helps in the process. Matching voice tone or tempo to that of the person I'm talking to, controlling body language, posture and gesture is also important.

Taking a genuine interest in other people, being curious about who they are and how they think and being willing to see the world from their point of view also makes them more receptive.

All this is done almost automatically and naturally. I consider myself lucky for not having any problems in establishing rapport with others.

Have you ever worked for a superior who was younger or less experienced than yourself?

I haven't worked for such a superior. My former superiors were very experienced professionals who were older than myself, from whom I've learned a lot. I don't consider age so important, what matters is a person's credibility, professionalism and competency.

How will you cope being supervised by someone younger or very much older than yourself?

I am comfortable working with any age group. I am far more interested in their qualities as a supervisor than in their age.

Or

I don't consider age so important, what matters is a person's credibility, professionalism and competency.

Or

I think it can be highly beneficial to have a mix of ages and types of experience – it provides a good opportunity for learning.

Are you able to work alone without direct supervision?
Owing to the nature of my occupation and the kind of tasks that I carry out in my job, I work independently on a regular basis. I am a self starter and don't need constant reassurance. I can set my own goals, or I can take assigned goals and complete them. I'm inner directed and enjoy applying my creativity and problem solving skills to my work. However, I'm not one of those individuals who will keep doing something wrong rather than seeking help. It's better to ask twice than loose your way once.

Hypothetical Questions

These kinds of questions present candidates with difficult 'real-life' situations, where almost any answer can be challenged. Bear in mind: if you are not cabin crew yet, you cannot really be expected to know the best reply - so do not be tricked into entering into an argument with an interviewer! A good way to approach these questions is to consider the feelings of all involved - and think about the implications for your colleagues and the airline as well.

Prove to your recruiters that you would be 'proactive' and do you best to resolve the situation using your own initiative - whilst remembering that you could ask for the help of more experienced crew if necessary. If you have followed these guidelines, and are still challenged, your interviewer may be testing your ability to manage conflict or stress. In either case it is important to remain calm, focused, and to demonstrate that although you appreciate there are many aspects to each situation, you would always be trying to find acceptable solutions.

What would you do if a commercially important passenger complained about a crying child?
I would apologise to the passenger and offer my assistance to the guardian of the crying child. I would be proactive and do my best to resolve the situation using my own initiative – whilst remembering that I can ask for the help of more experienced crew if necessary.

If you were given the job of interviewing Cabin Crew for XYZ Airlines, how would you do it?
If I had the job of picking cabin crew, I would look for desirable traits such as:

An approachable and friendly personality
Teamwork and customer care skills
Good communication and admin skills
An ability to work under pressure
A spirit of enthusiasm, confidence and a sense of humour.
The ability to manage change and adversity
Good listener and problem solver

These are the qualities I feel are necessary for the position.

What would you do if you suspect that a passenger is suspicious or a high risk to passengers?
I would report to the senior any abnormal behaviour, indicating a suspicious passenger.

What do you consider suspicious behaviour?
I consider someone who is fidgety, constantly looking around and being anxious to be suspicious behaviour.

What would you do and how would you react in a hijacking?
I'm sure there is a corporate policy for dealing with this situation and I will follow it.

How would you act in an emergency/How do you deal with a crisis?
I treat a crisis like a crisis. I move quickly, confidently, and authoritatively in those situations where decisive action is required.

What is the definition of an emergency?
An emergency is 'when something unexpected happens that requires major decisions to be made, quickly.'

How would you act in an emergency such as a crash landing?
As soon as I get the warning that something is going to happen, I would get a plan together in my mind. I would stay calm and in control and follow the emergency guidelines and procedures.

How would you handle a colleague who is being rude, racist, etc.?
If there is a corporate policy, I will follow it, if not; I will warn the person the first time and make it clear that this sort of behaviour is not on. If he or she continues, I would then report it to proper authority.

If you spotted a colleague doing something unethical or illegal, what would you do?
I would act immediately to put a stop to any unethical or illegal activity. I would try to document the details of the incident and try to collect any physical evidence. Then I would report it to my senior.

What three items would you choose to have if trapped on a desert island?
The 3 items I would have to have would be a medical kit containing various medicines, water purification tablets, surgical blades, plasters and cotton wool, etc. Second, I would have my survival kit containing essential items such as a compass, a striker and flint, a torch, waterproof matches, tallow candles (for eating, melting and frying), a magnifying glass, fish hooks and line. Third, a survival pouch containing fuel tablets, flexible saw, signal flares, a radio transmitter, brew kit and food.

Each 3 items are light-weight, conveniently small and can enable you to deal with a multitude of tasks.

If you were trapped on a desert island, what book would you want and why?
I would have to have my pocket sized 'Collins Gem, SAS survival guide', by John Wiseman. The guide is packed full of practical advice on survival in the wild, containing everything from attracting attention to yourself so that rescuers may find you to making your way across unknown territory back to civilisation if there is no hope of rescue.

There is essential information about navigating without a map or compass, maintaining your morale and that of others who share your situation, what to eat, how to take everything possible from nature and use it to the full, and how to maintain a healthy physical condition, or if sick or wounded heal yourself and others.

If you were going to Mars, what 3 items would you take?
First, an expert in the field. Second, sufficient oxygen to allow me to breathe in that environment. And finally, enough fuel for the return trip.

What would you do if you received a telephone call telling you that a family member has been taken ill in the middle of the day?
I would ring home, at the earliest convenience, to find out what the situation was. If it was something extremely serious (life or death situation), then I would hope that my employer would understand the need for me to take time off work at the earliest convenience. If on the other hand, the situation were not so serious, I would continue with my work as necessary.

You are in flight at 30,000 feet, how would you handle a passenger if he became irate about his lost baggage?

At 30,000 feet, there is not a lot you can do about the baggage so, the problem at hand is reassuring the passenger and avoiding further disruption. First, I would manoeuvre the passenger somewhere more private and sit him down, if possible. I would then ask him to quietly tell me about the situation, I would then apologise for the mishandling and offer to assist on the ground by escorting him to the proper people who can help.

What would you do if the seat belt signs are on because of turbulence, but a passenger gets up to go desperately to the toilet?

That is a new area for me, so I am afraid I can't really answer that, but I enjoy acquiring new knowledge and I do learn quickly.

Or

I'm sure there is a corporate policy for dealing with this situation and I will follow it.

Or

In non fatal accidents, turbulence is the biggest cause of injuries to both passengers and crew. Therefore I would suggest that the passenger wait until the seatbelt signs are turned off. If the passenger really cannot wait, I may seek the advice of a senior member of crew.

How would you handle a passenger who is intoxicated?

I would not provide any more alcoholic drinks; I would encourage food and offer a cup of tea or coffee. If the situation does not improve but instead worsens and the situation is out of my control, I would inform my senior and seek assistance from the other crew members.

You have a doctors appointment arranged, you have waited 2 weeks to get it, an urgent meeting is scheduled at the last moment, what do you do?

If it is not a life or death situation, then I would reschedule the appointment. I would then make sure I was properly prepared for the meeting.

What would you do if you felt your superior was dishonest/incompetent/had a personal problem?

That would depend on the seriousness of the problem and whether or not it was affecting his ability to do his job. Obviously in the case of dishonesty or incompetence, action would be required. A personal problem might or might not affect others in the workplace and I would need to make a judgement on the individual case.

What action would you take if the problem was affecting his ability to do his job or others ability to do theirs?

Only if the problem was that serious, I would report it to someone who could correct and rectify the situation.

What if I told you that your presentation this afternoon was lousy?

First of all, I would ask which aspects of my presentation were lousy. My next step would be to find out where you felt the problem was. If there was miscommunication, I'd clear it up. If the problem was elsewhere, I would seek your advice and be sure that the problem was not recurrent.

How would you deal with a passenger who is scared of flying?

I would go down to their level by kneeling next to where they are sitting, I would reassure the passenger that I understand and talk softly and calmly, talking them through the flight and reassuring them of any strange noises they may hear.

Being aware of what to expect will help keep those worries in check. Just realising that a planes wings are supposed to flex, to move around gently in flight, can help. Similarly, the collection of bumps and bangs that always accompany flight can be made less fearsome if they are expected. I would tell them where I can be found and show them the call bell. And finally say I will check on them during the flight

What do you do when a colleague comes to you in tears?

Naturally, I would take them aside and figure out what it was that was upsetting them so. If it were something that I could help with – for example getting them over a difficult deadline – I would try to offer them my time. But if it was a personal problem, I would try to listen and offer my support and shoulder to cry on.

What do you do when a co-worker is not pulling their weight?

I've noticed that such people simply lack enthusiasm and confidence, and that energetic and cheerful co workers can often change that. So when I feel others are not pulling their weight, I first try to overcome it with a positive attitude that I hope will catch on, if this does nothing, I will try to reason with and challenge the person. Failing that, I will need to consider seeking advice from a senior member of staff.

Technical Questions

In this context 'technical' questions are defined as those that have clear and factual answers. They reveal very little about personal qualities, except that a candidate has made the effort to find something out about the airline or plan their future.

It would be a good idea to do some basic research, and find out who the airline's chairman is, the history of the airline, the destinations operated, awards won and any recent initiatives (especially if they have been advertised, or have appeared in the news).

CAREER GOALS AND FUTURE PROGRESSION

Why do you want to be a Cabin Crew member/Why would you be happy doing this type of work?
Besides the fact that being a member of Cabin Crew has always been a lifelong ambition of mine, being a member of Cabin Crew also offers everything I'm looking for, both in the position itself and in the overall environment.

I want a job that offers not the normal nine to five, but something which is more varied, that allows me to contribute in different areas and work and meet with a wider range of people and cultures.

Being a member of cabin crew, I could use the customer care skills I have developed over the course of my career to deliver the standard of service that passengers expect and be sufficiently challenged to develop further whilst learning from new people, processes and clients.

I feel that for the above reasons I would be successful as cabin crew and would be a valuable asset to XYZ Airlines.

How did you become interested in the position of Cabin Crew/the travel industry?

I have always been interested in cabin crew, in anything to do with travel really. I grew up around aviation, my father worked at Any Aerospace and because of his work, we lived very close to the airport. This is where my passion for flying initially started. But it wasn't until I carried out a career suitability test at school that I really started to consider cabin crew as a serious future prospect. The test examined personal attributes, goals and skills and the final result came back suggesting suitability for the occupation. Based on this, I done a little more research into the job and agreed. This seems to be a job for which I am suited and is one I will feel committed to. I believe I can make the best contribution to a company by being happy at what I do.

Have you applied for any other positions?

At this stage, the position of cabin crew is the only position of interest that fits both my skills and career aspirations.

How will you adapt to returning to full time employment after working independently?

Being cabin crew is something I've always wanted to do and I have prepared myself for the transition. I enjoy the challenge of learning about and adapting to a new environment. That's one of the reasons I am seeking to make a change right now. I do not anticipate any problems adapting.

How have you prepared yourself for the transition?

I have prepared myself through the research I have done, the skills and experience I have acquired.

Can we take it then that you do still wish us to consider you for this post?

Certainly! Having had this chance to meet you and learn more about your operation and what the post will entail, I am even keener than before. I am convinced that this is the opportunity I am seeking and I know I can make a contribution.

Would you take this job if we offered it to you?

Yes, definitely. I was keen as soon as I saw the job opening on the web site. More than that though, actually meeting potential colleagues and finding out more about your current activities has clarified still further what an exciting challenge it would be to work here.

When are you available to start work if offered the position?
I have the energy and enthusiasm to start straight away. All I need is a weeks notice and I'm ready.

What would you say if I said your skills and experience were way below the requirements of this job?
I would ask what particular aspects of my skills and experience you felt were lacking and address each one of those areas with examples of where my skills and experiences do match your requirements. I would expect that after this discussion you would be left in no doubt about my ability to do this job.

If you were to leave the flight department, where would you turn your skills?
If for any reason, I was to leave the flight department, I would turn my skills to cabin crew training, or possibly airport personnel.

How would you respond if we told you that you have been unsuccessful on this occasion/How would you feel and what would you do if didn't secure a position with us today?
Naturally it will be a disappointment if I do not secure this job today because it is something I really want, I feel ready for it and I have had plenty of experience to contribute. However, I am not one to give up quickly; I will think about where I went wrong and how I could have done better, at the same time, I would take steps towards strengthening my candidacy.

How long have you been looking for a new position?
I have only recently started looking for a new position; this is my first application and interview.

Why have you decided to change professions at this stage of your career?
This career turnaround hasn't come suddenly. I have always liked this profession and have been gradually mastering the skills needed to perform its tasks. I am now ready to assume the responsibility and start achieving results.

How do you feel about looking for another job?
Looking for another job is an opportunity. I don't have to be looking for another job; I do it so that I can continue to grow professionally.

How important is job security to you?

Security is a basic need, but I know that there are no guarantees in life. The only true job security comes from making a meaningful contribution to my employer. If I know my job will be around for as long as I excel at it, I am able to concentrate on my work and remain focused.

How long would you stay with us?

I'm a loyal sort of person, and I don't like changing more than I need to. If the job is as challenging as I'm sure it is, and the opportunities for development within your organisation are as good as I believe they are, it may well be a career long commitment.

Or

I approach every new job with a long-term view. I would like to think that I can make a positive contribution to XYZ Airlines for the foreseeable future.

When do you expect a promotion/What do you think determines progress?

That depends on a few criteria. Of course, I cannot expect a promotion without the performance that marks me as deserving the promotion. I would like my career to continue progressing as well as it has in the past, but I'm a realist. I know promotions aren't given, they're earned. When I've mastered the position, improved it with my ideas, and prepared myself to take on new responsibilities, I'll be ready for a promotion.

How important to you is the opportunity to reach the top?

Reaching the top is a very relative term, but if by reaching the top you mean being a top performer and being successful in my occupation, I do consider reaching the top as very important.

How much thought have you given to your future?

Essentially, I have given my career and opportunities a great deal of thought, but business changes so rapidly these days, it's hard to plan precisely. But I do know I want to get ahead in the airline industry and I think the opportunities to do that in this airline are excellent.

Where do you picture yourself in 5 years/What are your long term career objectives?

This is a lively and expanding company by all accounts, so I very much hope that I shall be here in 5 years time. My job will have increased at least one possibly two levels in responsibility and scope and I'll have become a thorough professional with a clear understanding of the industry and company. I'll have made a significant contribution and will be working on new ways to further my career. By this time, my goals for the long term should be sharply defined.

So you don't yet have any long term plans?

I'm certainly ambitious, and I like to keep moving and progressing, but I find it's far more rewarding to let the job lead me forward.

What goals do you have?

My general goal is to do everything possible to keep learning and expanding my knowledge and skills. Beyond that, my goal is to maintain optimum health through exercise and a proper diet.

How will this job help you reach your career goals?

I am consistently striving to increase my knowledge and skills and I believe that this position can offer me a real step up in terms of challenge and experience. I feel that my present career plans would be more than fulfilled by this role. The position would allow me to use the skills I already have, but be sufficiently challenging to give the opportunity for further development.

What steps have you already taken to achieve your goals?

One of the most significant steps I've taken is applying for this job. The position could be significant for my future development, experience and knowledge.

Would you like to have my job?

Only for the next ten minutes so that I could hire myself.

Are you're present career objectives different from your original goals?

No; I have always wanted to get into this profession and through all the positions I have worked, I have been gradually mastering the skills needed to perform its tasks. I am now ready to assume the responsibility and start achieving results.

Describe the perfect job/What would you consider to be the ideal job for you?
The perfect job is one that offers daily challenges, provides the kind of stimulation that keeps my skills and abilities at peak levels, and allows me to achieve tangible results on a regular basis – something that is fast paced, in a situation where new ideas and creativity are fostered.

What do you want out of your life?
I want a successful career, personal development and good health.

So you wouldn't like an easy life, where you didn't need to work/Would you work if you suddenly became a millionaire/Why do you work?
I don't have any desire for an easy life. I suppose an easy life would be nice for a while, but then I would become restless. I'm interested in achievement, accomplishment, and seeing just how much I can do with the talent and intelligence I have. My career remains my first priority.

Or

Working is about more than the money, it's about having something meaningful to do, a reason to wake up in the morning, problems to solve, goals to accomplish, this is what life is all about to me. I suppose a life of luxury would be nice for a while, but then I would become restless. My career remains my first priority.

XYZ AIRLINES

Why do you want to work for XYZ Airlines/What interests you most about XYZ Airlines/Why did you select XYZ Airlines?
The safety record and outstanding reputation of XYZ Airlines was a significant factor that influenced my decision to apply. When people think of XYZ Airlines, they know what they are getting – a consistently high and reliable service and an airline that cares about their customers, this fact is also demonstrated by the many awards that the airline has received.

Also, I have flown with XYZ Airlines in the past and was very impressed with the service I received. As well as projecting an excellent image, I see a vibrant, responsive organisation with great potential for growth, and I want to be part of it.

I know that I'll be able to contribute to the airlines future success.

Have you ever flown with XYZ Airlines/ What do you think about the way we run our operation?
I flew with XYZ Airlines from London to California in October 2004. I had always heard so many wonderful things about the airline and had to try you out.

Onboard, the service was excellent and I felt like I was flying first class. The meal was outstanding, about the best you'll find anywhere ... The seats were comfortable and the in-flight entertainment was impressive, with a variety to choose from.

As for the crew, they really take care of all their passengers and they do everything to make the flight as pleasant as possible. They are attentive, competent and very friendly and fun to talk to, and always smiling.

XYZ Airlines really are a classy airline and deserve to be the best airline in the world.

What is the worst thing you have heard about XYZ Airlines?
The worst thing I have heard about this organisation is that competition for jobs is fierce because it is a terrific company. Every thing else I have heard, have been impressively positive.

How long would it take you to make a contribution to XYZ Airlines?
I would predict that I will make an immediate contribution to XYZ Airlines. Training is a factor and it takes time to learn, but it's not necessary to wait until after training has been completed to make a contribution.

Do you have any reservations about working here?
I see this position as a fine opportunity and the airline as one I would be proud to be a member of. I don't have any reservations at this point and I wouldn't be applying to join you if I did.

If one of our competitors offered you a job now, would you take it?
Because I want to work as cabin crew, if I did not get this job with XYZ Airlines, then I would have to consider other airlines. However, XYZ Airlines are my first and best choice.

How would you describe the ideal airline?
The ideal airline is a progressive, forward-thinking one that provides a challenging, stimulating and supporting atmosphere for its employees and their achievements. People enjoy working there and give their best to achieve the company's goals and targets.

Have you applied to any other airlines?
I have researched other airlines that would interest me but, after researching the history, development and future plans of XYZ Airlines, along with meeting people who work here, it seems like a perfect fit. I really appreciate what XYZ Airlines has to offer in the way of growth potential, and good reputation and I would really like to work for you, so although it is taking a bit of a risk, I wanted to see how things went with my application to you, before I considered applying to any other airlines.

Or

Although I am set on making cabin crew my future career, making a job change is a major decision, a long term commitment that I take very seriously, therefore the job I take, and the people I work with have got to have values that I can identify with. I'm very choosy about the airlines I approach and have not found such an interesting airline as this so far.

How would you rate us against our competitors?
It's so difficult to be objective, and I really don't like to slight your competition.

If probed further
Because I haven't flown with any of your major competitors it would be difficult for me to make any comparisons. However, from my research and talking to people who have flown with these airlines, it appears that XYZ Airlines has the best reputation, in the way of safety record and providing customer care. XYZ Airlines is recognised as being one of the worlds leading airlines.

How would you compare XYZ Airlines to the other airlines you have flown with?

My experiences with each of the airlines I have flown with have all been good and I never had a problem or cause for complaint. However, an advantage of XYZ Airlines is the diversity of the crew - I have never had such an excellent crew like on your flights. They really take care of all their passengers and do everything to make the flight as pleasant as possible. They are attentive, competent and very friendly and fun to talk to, and always smiling.

With XYZ Airlines, I really felt like I was flying first class. The meal was outstanding, about the best you'll find anywhere - the seats were comfortable and the in-flight entertainment was very impressive, with a wide variety to choose from.

XYZ Airlines really are a classy airline and deserve the 'airline of the year award'.

Do you think XYZ Airlines has a good reputation?

During my research into your airline, I did not come across any information that indicated a bad reputation, in fact quite the contrary, you seem to have a very good reputation.

What have you come across that indicates a good reputation?

According to reports on airlines, XYZ Airlines has surpassed many airlines on accreditations and awards which indicates and proves beyond all doubt that XYZ Airlines has an excellent reputation and leads the way within the airline industry.

Is there any way in which you think we can improve our service?

From my research into the airline industry, I have noticed that some airlines are introducing new trends. Such as massage therapy and beauty salons on board their planes. I think this is a good idea for XYZ Airlines to consider, if it has not already been considered.

Is there anything you think we do badly?

I haven't come across anything to suggest that you are doing anything badly, in fact, quite the opposite. Plus I am sure you wouldn't enjoy your current success if you were doing anything really wrong and I wouldn't be applying to join you if that were the case.

What do you look for in an airline?
I look for a good reputation in an active, creative and stimulating environment where I am limited only by my capabilities and where positive results are acknowledged. I believe XYZ Airlines offers all of this and more.

How do you research the airlines you wish to work for?
First, I search the airlines website to learn more about the position, responsibilities and potential for growth, I then find out about their reputation, and visit the airline to meet the people who already work there and assess the overall environment.

This position will involve relocating, how will you adjust to the different lifestyle?
I realise that this position involves transfers and I bore that in mind when I applied. I am fully aware of what to expect from the research I have done about any destination, and having visited the destination, I welcome the different lifestyle.

Or

I like England, but for this opportunity I am happy to relocate. I am fully aware of what to expect from the research I have done and would welcome the different lifestyle.

Do you feel appearance is important?
Yes, to a certain extent. Appearance is important in the sense that you should be neat, clean and tidy. Your appearance contributes to whether people will have the confidence in you – and the ability to inspire confidence is a great asset.

Whilst appearance is an important factor, so is tone of voice, manner, and behaviour important.

How would I know you were under pressure?
I disguise my pressure well; therefore you wouldn't know if I were under pressure.

What question could I ask you that would really intimidate you?
I can't think of any question that would intimidate me; this is probably the most intimidating question.

What have you done that shows initiative and willingness to work/At Any Hair Salon, what did you do in your job that was not covered by your job description?
To achieve peak performance, I always put in more effort than merely doing the job by the book. This comes naturally to me, as part of my work ethics. I am not happy with mediocre efforts because they lead to mediocre results.

At Any Hair Salon, to achieve goals and produce results, I sometimes performed various tasks that were not, strictly speaking, a part of my job. By doing more than required, I not only learn more, I also become more efficient and productive. If I'm able to do the task, instead of waiting for the job to be done, I simply do it.

For example…When I first began working at Any Hair Salon, the inventory system was outdated, and the storage room was very messy and disorganised, so I came in on my day off, cleaned up the mess, organised the store cupboards, and catalogued it all on the new inventory forms. Thereafter when orders arrived, it was easy to organise and therefore retrieve.

Under what circumstances do you seek help?

I am aware of my own strengths but I am also prepared to ask for help from people with specialist knowledge.

If there is not much time and I need little help, I will seek assistance. Also, if I am confused, I will seek help – it's better to ask a dumb question than make a stupid mistake.

What kind of things do you worry about/what keeps you up at night?

I think worrying is pretty pointless – I prefer to take action and make changes. I have concerns, obviously – but for the most part I feel that I am in control of my life. However, areas that do concern me are meeting deadlines, reaching sales targets and getting supplies on time; just the normal stuff. But I wouldn't say that these things trouble me overly.

How would you rate me as an interviewer?

First, I'd give you high marks for your people skills. You helped me feel at ease right away, which made it easier for me to answer the questions. I'd also rate you highly on the creativity of the questions and their thoroughness. By probing me as carefully as you have, you've given me a better opportunity to secure this position. You've given me a complete picture of what to expect at XYZ Airlines, and it confirms my belief that this is where I want to work.

How do you feel about company rules and policies?

I consider company rules, policies and procedures necessary for the efficient running of any business. They ensure that fairness, consistency and safety measures are applied across the board and that the right work environment is created and maintained. They help people make decisions and give them a sense of direction. My personal policy is always to observe the rules and make sure my colleagues observe them as well.

Have you ever felt constraints /have you ever had to go against those traditions and policies to reach your goal?

We all feel the constraints of some policies and procedures from time to time. However, to achieve uniformity and consistency and to ensure that relevant standards and regulations are followed, it is necessary to have those policies and procedures in place. It is always possible to cut corners and achieve the required results sooner or with less effort, but I have never taken the path of least resistance.

To get the job done people sometimes have to bend the truth. Give me an example when you had to do the same thing.

No I have never bent the truth and have always abided by company policies. I believe this is key to being a professional and successful employee.

No matter how much you are probed, do not give in.

Have you stretched the truth today to gain a favourable outcome?

No, I haven't tried to be someone I am not, because I wouldn't want to get the job that way. To win that way would be such a short term gain because eventually I would be found out.

You know what we're prepared to pay for this position, would you be prepared to take it for this figure?

Salary is not the most important thing as far as I'm concerned. I'm more concerned about finding the right job and the right employer. I'm sure the salary wouldn't prove to be a problem.

What do you think you should be earning in 5 years?

I hope that my pay will reflect my contribution to the organisation, but the most important thing for me is job satisfaction and compatibility with the team I work with and the company I work for.

HAVEN'T EXPERIENCED THE SITUATION, ETC.

If you are really stuck and cannot answer a question, or if you haven't experienced a situation that you are being asked about, then it is best to say so. A quietly confident admission is more impressive than trying to bluff your way through or saying nothing at all.

- No. I am pleased to say, that is not an experience I have had to go through.
- I am sorry, but that isn't an area I am familiar with at present, so I can't really give you any details on that.
- I am sorry, but I haven't come across that particular term before, would you mind clarifying it for me.
- I am not familiar with that particular system, though I would imagine it is quite similar to others that I have used and I am usually quick at getting to grips with new systems.
- That is a new area for me, so I am afraid I can't really answer that, but I enjoy acquiring new knowledge and I do learn quickly.
- Sorry, I've never been in that situation. I could imagine my response if you like.
- Sorry, I can't remember ever being in that situation, but I did face something slightly similar that I could discuss.
- I've never been in that situation, but assuming I was successful and working for you, I think I'd handle it like this ___.
- That's a tough question; I need time to think about my answer. Can we come back to it later?
- That's an interesting question, may I have a moment or two to collect my thoughts.
- There is quite a lot I could say about that, can you bear with me while I think about that for a minute.
- I am not sure where I should start with that, please would you give me a little bit more of an explanation.
- Sorry, I'm not sure I understand, could you repeat the question please.

QUESTIONS FOR THE INTERVIEWERS

The questions you ask the recruiters can say a lot about you and what you know about the airline and the position itself. Therefore, it is a good idea to prepare one or two intelligent questions in advance.

Your list of questions needs to follow these guidelines:

- Don't ask questions that could be easily answered through your own research.
- Ask questions which demonstrate a genuine interest in and knowledge of the Airline and the position.
- Your questions should also demonstrate that you know just that little bit more than is required. Sort of bonus features if they take you on.

Below are some good examples of the sorts of questions you could ask.

- How did you get into this industry/Why did you choose to work for XYZ Airlines?
- What is it about this Airline that keeps you here?
- It sounds as if you really enjoy working here, what have you enjoyed most about working for XYZ Airlines?
- Is there anything else I need to do to maximise my chances of getting this job?
- How soon after being successful would I begin training?
- I am looking for a long term career with you and if I am lucky enough to be offered the position, what opportunities would there be for promotion in the future?
- Do you have any reservations about my ability to do this job/What do you foresee as possible obstacles or problems I might have?
  This is a good question to ask as the interviewer will disclose their concerns. You can then follow up to reassure the interviewer... You could say something like 'Thank you. That has been very helpful, perhaps then it would be helpful for you to know that ____.'

No Questions.
I did have plenty of questions, but we've covered them all during our discussions. I was particularly interested in __, but we've dealt with that thoroughly.

I had many questions, but you've answered them all you've been so helpful. I'm even more excited about this opportunity than when I applied.

Background

Personal Details

69   How would the job impact your family/home life?
69   This position requires long hours, will this be a problem for your social/family life?
69   What do your family think about you applying for this position/your chosen career?

Outside interests

69   What do you do to relax after a hard day?
70   What have you achieved through your interests?
70   What is your energy level like/Where do you get your energy from?
70   Your interests appear rather solitary, cycling, swimming, running, reading, yoga etc. How do you think this reflects your personality?

Education and training

School

71   I see You studied French at school, what is your fluency?
70   What subjects gave you the most difficulty?
71   What subjects were the easiest for you?
70   What were your favourite subjects?
70   Why didn't you do better in your exams?
71   Why didn't you stay on at school or continue full time education/ Do you feel you made the right choice?

Co-workers

75 How do superiors get the best out of you?

74 Tell us about your last work group/Did you get along with your co workers?

75 What did you dislike about your superiors? How could your superiors have done a better job?

Present Employment

79 What characteristics (personal qualities and skills) are necessary for success working freelance?

78 How do you define doing a good job in your profession?

79 How do you maintain your interest in your work?

79 How would you compare the quality of your work to your competitors/other hairdressers?

79 How would you compare the quantity of your work to your competitors/other hairdressers?

78 In what areas of your current work are you strongest?

78 In what areas of your current work are you weakest?

77 In what ways are you prepared for the career and lifestyle change?

80 Is there a lot of pressure in your current work/How do you deal with this pressure?

81 What are some of the problems you encounter in your work/Can you think of a problem you encountered in your current job and the steps you took to overcome it/ Tell us about some obstacles you had to overcome in the past?

79 What characteristics (personal qualities and skills) are necessary for success working as a hairdresser?

76 What do you dislike about your current job/What is the worst part of the job?

75 What do you like about your current job?

80 What have you done to make your work more challenging?

80 What have you done to make your work more effective?

80 What have you done to make your work more interesting?

76 What have you enjoyed least about working freelance/your current job?

76 What have you enjoyed most about working freelance/your current job?

80 What is the most important thing about the work you do?

Work Experience General

Professional knowledge and experience

85 What is the most significant accomplishment/achievement up to this point in your career?

85 In your current/past position, what problems did you come across that came as a surprise to you?

85 In your current/past position, what problems did you identify that had been previously overlooked?

86 When have you experienced a pressured situation/Tell us about a time when you have been pressured by an awkward or difficult person/Tell us about a time when you have had to be assertive/When have you had to say no to a client?

87 Tell us about a difficult situation when you pulled the team together/Describe a situation when the team fell apart. What was your role in the outcome?

87 Tell us about a time when you have been pressured by an awkward or difficult person?

88 What was the most difficult situation you have faced/How did you cope/How did you feel?

88 What has been the biggest disappointment of your career?

89 Describe a time when you've had to deal with an angry or upset customer/How did you resolve the situation?

89 Tell us about a time when you were confronted by someone shouting at or being abusive toward you/How did you cope/How did this make you feel?

90 What has been your greatest professional mistake/What was the biggest mistake you have ever made?

90 How have you benefited/learned from your mistakes?

91 How have you benefited/learned from your disappointments?

91 How do you prepare yourself for potential problems?

91 What do you do when you have trouble solving a problem?

91 How do you handle failure?

91 What have been the biggest frustrations in your career?

92 How do you approach difficult situations?

92 How often have you missed deadlines and what were the outcomes?

92 Give me an example of a problem you encountered that didn't work out

92 Tell us about a time when you solved a customer problem

93 Please briefly relate an experience where you were especially pleased with the service/assistance you were able to give someone/When have you gone out of your way for a client?

Skills & Abilities

Personal traits and skills

My Views

101 Name 5 things that motivate you

99 Rate yourself on a scale from 1 to 10

100 Tell us about a time when you have had to be assertive?

103 What are some of the things that bother you?

107 What are some of the things you find difficult to do?

107 What are the 3 most important skills that you have developed in your career so far?

98 What are your 3 greatest strengths and weaknesses?

97 What are your best qualities/greatest strengths?

108 What are your dislikes?

108 What are your likes?

108 What do you consider yourself good at doing?

100 What do you do when you find it difficult to do your best work?

107 What don't you like to do?

109 What is your most memorable characteristic/What makes you stand out from the crowd?

103 What makes you angry/Tell us about the last time you felt angry/What makes you impatient/Tell us about the last time you felt impatient.

101 What motivates you to work hard?

97 What qualities are you not so proud of/ What is your greatest weakness?

110 What would you say is your leadership style?

101 When do you tend to do your best work, in the morning or in the afternoon?

102 When have you had to face major changes in your personal life or work?

99 Would you classify yourself as a hard-working or relatively laid back?

Other People's Views

111 Do you have a competitive nature?

111 How well did superiors rate your job performance/ What did superiors think are your strengths/ In what areas have you received compliments from superiors?

110 How would a friend describe you?

110 How would an enemy describe your character?

112 What did superiors think are your weaknesses?

111 What would colleagues say about you/What do other people think of the way you work/What do others think are your best qualities/strengths?

Communication/Interpersonal skills

- *114* How confident are you about addressing a group?
- *114* How do you handle conflict/If you have a disagreement with a colleague, how do you handle it?
- *112* How important is communication when dealing with your clients?
- *114* Tell us about a time that you had to be tactful
- *113* What action do you take if there are members of your team who really don't get on with one another, to the point where this is affecting other staff and performance?
- *113* What was the toughest communication problem you have faced?
- *112* When have you shown good communication/interpersonal skills?

Decision making

- *115* Do you consider yourself to be thoughtful and analytical or do you usually make up your mind fast?
- *116* How do you go about making important decisions?
- *115* What decisions do you dislike making?
- *115* What decisions do you find most difficult?
- *115* What was the most difficult decision you have made?

General Motives & Perceptions

Knowledge and Suitability for the job

Cabin Crew

- *119* Are you willing to start as a trainee?
- *124* Do you feel confident in your ability to handle this position?
- *124* Do you feel ready for a more responsible position/In what ways has your work experience prepared you to take on greater responsibility?
- *119* Do you know anything about Cabin Crew training?
- *120* Do you think the role of cabin crew is glamorous?
- *124* Do you think your lack of language skills will affect your ability to perform the job?
- *126* Have you worked on night shifts before?
- *126* How do you feel about a formal dress code?
- *126* How do you feel about living out of a suitcase?

120	How do you feel about the 6 month probationary period?
125	How do you feel about working at Christmas, and other special occasions?
123	How is your work experience related to Cabin Crew/How has your work experience prepared you for the role?
127	How will you adapt your behaviour to the wide range of ethnic differences?
126	How will you cope with the wide range of ethnic differences/How do you feel about working in a very multi-cultural environment, colleagues and customers?
121	If you could, what would you change about this position?
125	This is a long hours culture, is that a problem for you?
124	What challenges do you anticipate from this position?
123	What challenges do you look forward to?
127	What contribution can you make to ensure passengers will fly with us again?
121	What do you expect from this job?
123	What do you hope to achieve from this position/What do you wish to gain at XYZ Airlines?
121	What do you think are the advantages of the position?
120	What do you think are the disadvantages of this position/How will you cope with the disadvantages/ What problems do you think you'll face in this job?
118	What do you think the role of cabin crew involves/What do you think is the primary responsibility of Cabin Crew?
124	What is it about being a Cabin Crew member that you think you do not presently have?
117	What kind of individual do you think we are looking for to fill this role?
123	What makes this job different from your current/previous ones/ What was the least relevant job you have held?
118	What qualities do you have that you feel would make you a good cabin crew member?
119	What qualities do you think a good Cabin Crew member should have/What do you think it takes to be a successful cabin crew member/How many of those qualities do you have?
121	What will you look forward to most in this job?

125   What would you bring to the position//In what ways will XYZ Airlines benefit from hiring you//I'm not sure you are suitable for the position, convince me.

122   Why should we hire you for this position rather than another applicant/I have a preferred candidate for this role, change my mind.

122   Why should we hire you instead of someone with prior Cabin Crew experience?

122   Why should we hire you?

121   Will you be able to cope with the change in environment?

General perceptions

128   Has anyone in the business world ever been an inspiration to you/Who was the most influential person in your life?

127   What is your idea of success/Define a successful career?

Perceptions About Customer Care

132   Do you think the customer is always right?

132   How would you deal with a passenger who is not right but believes he is right?

129   How would you define good customer service?

131   What aspects of customer service are most important to our passengers?

130   What do you find most challenging about providing customer service?

131   What do you most/least enjoy about providing customer care?

130   What do you think constitutes poor customer service?

131   What do you think is the main cause of some passenger's frustrations?

129   What is the key to providing good customer service?

130   When have you provided good customer service?

130   When have you thought that your customer service could have been better?

129   When have you witnessed poor customer service/When have you witnessed good customer service?

131   Why do you think some passengers take out their frustrations on Cabin Crew?

Perceptions About Teamwork & Working Relationships

Hypothetical Questions

Technical Questions

Career goals and future progression

XYZ Airlines

Miscellaneous

165   Do you feel appearance is important?

166   Have you ever felt constraints /have you ever had to go against those traditions and policies to reach your goal?

167   Have you stretched the truth today to gain a favourable outcome?

166   How do you feel about company rules and policies?

165   How would I know you were under pressure?

166   How would you rate me as an interviewer?

167   To get the job done people sometimes have to bend the truth. Give me an example when you had to do the same thing.

166   Under what circumstances do you seek help?

167   What do you think you should be earning in 5 years?

165   What have you done that shows initiative and willingness to work/At Any Hair Salon, what did you do in your job that was not covered by your job description?

166   What kind of things do you worry about/what keeps you up at night?

165   What question could I ask you that would really intimidate you?

167   You know what we're prepared to pay for this position, would you be prepared to take it for this figure?

Part 2b

Forms

In this part...

Application Record
Post Interview Worksheet
Notes

Application Record

Airline	Application Date	Interview Date

on record

Airline	Application Date	Interview Date

Post Interview Worksheet

Airline: _____   **Date:** _____

Interview location: _____

Recruiters: _____

What I did well:

What could have been improved?

Notes:

Airline: _____   Date: _____

Interview location: _____

Recruiters: _____

What I did well:

What could have been improved?

Notes:

Post Interview Worksheet

Airline: _____   **Date:** _____

Interview location: _____

Recruiters: _____

What I did well:

What could have been improved?

Notes:

Airline: _____ **Date:** _____

Interview location: _____

Recruiters: _____

What I did well:

What could have been improved?

Notes:

Post Interview Worksheet

Airline: _____ **Date:** _____

Interview location: _____

Recruiters: _____

What I did well:

What could have been improved?

Notes:

Airline: _____   Date: _____

Interview location: _____

Recruiters: _____

What I did well:

What could have been improved?

Notes:

Post Interview Worksheet

Airline: _____ Date: _____

Interview location: _____

Recruiters: _____

What I did well:

What could have been improved?

Notes:

Airline: _____   **Date:** _____

Interview location: _____

Recruiters: _____

What I did well:

What could have been improved?

Notes:

Notes

Notes

Notes